BY THE EDITORS OF CONSUMER GUIDE

FAVORITE BRAND NAME RECIPES

Appetizers, Dips & Party Snacks

BEEKMAN HOUSE
New York

Contents

Louis Weber, President
Publications International, Ltd.
3841 West Oakton Street
Skokie, Illinois 60076

Permission is never granted for commercial purposes.

Manufactured in the United States of America
10 9 8 7 6 5 4

Library of Congress Catalog Card Number: 82-82134
ISBN: 0-517-383659

This edition published by:
Beekman House
Distributed by Crown Publishers, Inc.
One Park Avenue
New York, New York 10016

Cover Design: Linda Snow Shum

Front Cover: 1. Ribbon Cubes; Wrap-Ups; Party Pinwheels; Hot Bacon Spread
Oscar Mayer & Co.

2. Spectacular Shrimp Spread
Gulf and South Atlantic Fisheries Development Foundation, Inc.

3. Pastrami Pizzas
Carl Buddig & Co.

Back Cover: Shrimp With Sweet-Sour Sauce; Chicken Kabobs
Kikkoman International, Inc.

Introduction

All of us made this recipe collection possible by taking certain recipes that first appeared on food product labels or in advertisements and choosing them as our favorites! We have included only quality recipes that are or will soon become family treasures. The recipes are reprinted exactly as they appear on the labels or in the advertisements.

The **APPETIZER** section is divided into two major categories—**Hot Appetizers** and **Cold Appetizers** with a section in each called **First Course Appetizers**—prepare these for a sit-down, more formal meal. For unexpected guests, go directly to the **Quick & Easy Appetizers** section.

DIPS & SPREADS have long been American favorites, and we have included the best—old and new! **PARTY SNACKS** include recipes to enjoy while watching TV or after returning from a football game, plus new and old recipes for Party Mixes and more.

The recipes in this book range in scope from gourmet style, such as "Elegant Crab Meat Balls," to old family favorites, like "California Dip." We have also included ethnic specialties, such as "Azteca® Nachos," "Party Pizzas" and "Mini Quiches."

To look up your favorite recipe in the **INDEX**, if you do not remember the exact title, look under the brand name or the main food ingredient, such as "cheese." Many Low Calorie, Low Cholesterol, Low Sodium and Low Fat recipes are included to help the diet watchers, and some Microwave recipes too.

For the convenience of our readers we have included an address directory of all food manufacturers listed in the book (see **ACKNOWLEDGMENTS**). Any questions or comments should be directed to the individual manufacturers for prompt attention. All recipes in this book have been copyrighted by the food manufacturers and cannot be reprinted without their permission. By printing these recipes, CONSUMER GUIDE® is *not* endorsing particular brand name foods.

Hot Appetizers

Crisco
Zippy Meatball Appetizers

1 egg, beaten
¾ cup soft bread crumbs (about 1 slice of bread)
¼ cup chili sauce
½ teaspoon salt
½ teaspoon instant minced onion
⅛ teaspoon garlic powder
¾ pound ground beef
⅓ cup **CRISCO®**
Bottle barbeque sauce

In a bowl, combine the egg, crumbs, chili sauce, salt, instant minced onion, and garlic powder. Add ground beef and mix thoroughly. Shape mixture into about 30 small meatballs. In large skillet, brown meatballs slowly on all sides in hot **CRISCO®**. Continue cooking till meatballs are done, shaking skillet to turn meatballs. Keep meatballs hot; serve on wooden picks and dip in warmed barbeque sauce.   *Makes about 30 meatballs*

Barbecued Miniature Meatballs

2 eggs, slightly beaten
½ cup water
1 envelope **FRENCH'S® Potato Pancake Mix**
1½ pounds ground beef
Barbecue Sauce*

Combine eggs, water, and contents of pancake mix envelope; let stand 10 minutes. Add ground beef; mix lightly. Shape small meatballs, using about 1 rounded teaspoonful for each; arrange in single layer on ungreased baking sheets. Bake in 400° oven 10 to 15 minutes, until done. Prepare Barbecue Sauce in chafing dish or skillet. Add meatballs. Serve with food picks.
Makes 50 to 75 hors d'oeuvres

*Barbecue Sauce

Combine 1 envelope **FRENCH'S® Sloppy Joe Seasoning Mix**, 6-oz. can tomato paste, 1½ cups water, 1 tablespoon brown sugar, and 2 tablespoons vinegar in small saucepan. Simmer 5 minutes, stirring occasionally.

Wyler's
Appetizer Meatball Paprikash

1 pound lean ground beef
¾ cup chopped onion
½ cup soft bread crumbs
1 egg
5 teaspoons **WYLER'S® Beef-Flavor Instant Bouillon**
2 tablespoons vegetable oil
3 tablespoons flour
1 tablespoon paprika
1¼ cups water
1½ teaspoons Worcestershire sauce
½ cup **BORDEN® Sour Cream**, at room temperature

In medium bowl, combine meat, ¼ cup onion, crumbs, egg and 1 **tablespoon** bouillon; mix well. Shape into 1¼-inch meatballs. In large skillet, brown meatballs in oil; remove from pan. Stir in remaining onion; cook until tender. Stir in flour and paprika then water, remaining bouillon and Worcestershire sauce. Cook and stir until thickened and smooth. Stir in sour cream. Add meatballs; stir to coat. Heat through. Serve hot with wooden picks. Refrigerate leftovers.   *Makes about 3 dozen*

Sweet and Sour Meatballs

Meatballs:
1½ lb. ground chuck
½ cup uncooked **WOLFF'S® Kasha** (buckwheat groats)
2 eggs, beaten
1 carrot, grated
1 medium onion, chopped
1 garlic clove, minced
1½ tsp. salt
2-3 Tbsp. oil

Sauce:
1 can (20 oz.) pineapple chunks, drained (save juice)
¾ cup reserved pineapple juice
½ cup water
2 Tbsp. cornstarch
1 beef bouillon cube
1 Tbsp. soy sauce
1 tsp. fresh ginger-root, grated or ½ tsp. ground ginger
¼ cup wine vinegar
¼ cup unsulphured molasses, honey, or sugar
1 green pepper, cut into chunks

Combine meatball ingredients except oil; shape into 4 dozen appetizer size meatballs. Brown meatballs on all sides in hot oil; drain on paper towels. Add to Sweet and Sour Sauce.

To prepare sauce: In saucepan, combine all ingredients except pineapple chunks and green pepper. Cook, stirring until thick and clear (about 5 minutes). Add meatballs, pineapple, and green pepper chunks. Heat until hot and meatballs are thoroughly cooked.

VARIATION:

Shape into 2 dozen meal-size meatballs. Serve over additional cooked kasha, noodles, or rice.

Holiday Meatballs

Meatballs:
2 pounds lean ground beef
1 tablespoon seasoned salt
1 tablespoon brown sugar
¾ cup water
2 teaspoons lemon peel
1 8-oz. package **BORDO Imported Diced Dates**

Sauce:
3 10¾ oz. cans condensed tomato soup
1½ soup cans of water
¾ cup brown sugar
3 tablespoons lemon juice
1 8-oz. package **BORDO Imported Diced Dates**

Meatballs: Mix ground beef and remaining meatball ingredients until well blended and dates are dispersed through mixture. Set aside.

Sauce: Place tomato soup in a large (5-6 quart), heavy saucepan. Add water, brown sugar and lemon juice. Mix well. Bring to a slow boil, uncovered, over medium heat. Then simmer. Stir occasionally.

Using about 1 teaspoon of meat mixture, shape with hands into balls and drop into simmering liquid. Repeat until meat mixture is

used. Simmer meatballs in sauce, uncovered, 15 minutes. Add dates. Mix carefully. Simmer an additional 15 minutes, stirring every 5 minutes, until sauce thickens.

Serves 8-10 as a hearty appetizer

Meatball Appetizer

1 pound ground beef
1 packet **HERB-OX® Low Sodium Beef-Flavored Instant Broth and Seasoning**
⅛ teaspoon cayenne pepper
½ cup fresh strawberries, washed and hulled
2 tablespoons peanut or vegetable oil

In a large bowl, mix the beef thoroughly with the packet of **HERB-OX® Low Sodium Beef-Flavored Instant Broth and Seasoning**, pepper and mashed strawberries. Roll meat into ping-pong sized balls and sauté in 2 tablespoons peanut or vegetable oil until crisp and browned. Serve with toothpicks. *Serves 6-8*

Square Meatballs

1 pound lean ground beef
1 egg
¾ cup fine soft bread crumbs
2 tablespoons ketchup
2 tablespoons water
½ teaspoon **LAWRY'S® Seasoned Salt**
½ teaspoon **LAWRY'S® Seasoned Pepper**
1 teaspoon **LAWRY'S® Minced Onions With Green Onion Flakes**

For Garnish:
Ripe olives, halved
Cocktail onions
Cheese wedges
Pickle slices

Mix together all ingredients except those used for garnish. Shape into a rectangle 8 × 6 × ½-inch on a jelly roll pan. Mark into 1-inch squares. Top each square with your choice of garnish. Bake in a 400° F oven 15 minutes. Cut into squares and use a wooden pick to serve each square. *Makes 4 dozen*

Sausage With Hot Mustard Sauce

8 ounce package **SWIFT PREMIUM® BROWN 'N SERVE™ Sausage Links**

Cut sausage links into halves. Brown according to package directions. Keep hot on hot tray or in chafing dish. Spear sausage pieces with smooth wooden picks. Serve with Hot Mustard Sauce* for a dip. *Yield: 20 appetizers*

(Continued)

*Hot Mustard Sauce

2 tablespoons butter or margarine
1 tablespoon flour
½ teaspoon salt
1 cup water
1 beef bouillon cube
⅓ cup Dijon-style mustard
2 teaspoons horseradish
2 tablespoons sugar

Melt butter in a saucepan. Stir in flour and salt. Gradually add water. Add bouillon cube, mustard, horseradish and sugar. Stir and cook until sauce thickens. *Yield: 1½ cups*

Appetizer Franks With Mustard Sauce

Mustard Sauce*
1 lb. WILSON® Western Grillers or Jumbo Franks

Prepare mustard sauce. Keep warm. Cut each frank into 6 pieces. Place in baking pan. Bake in 350°F oven 5 minutes or until heated through. Serve with toothpicks. *48 appetizer servings*

*Mustard Sauce

Place ¾ cup evaporated milk and ¼ lb. sliced American cheese in a small saucepan. Heat over medium heat, stirring constantly, until cheese is melted. Stir in ¼ cup prepared mustard until smooth. Keep warm.

Vienna Beef® Saucy Franks

1 lb. VIENNA BEEF® Cocktail Franks
1 10½ oz. can condensed tomato soup
1 cup water
1 medium onion, chopped
½ tsp. salt
⅛ tsp. pepper

Preheat oven to 350°. Place franks in baking dish. Combine remaining ingredients and pour over franks. Bake, covered, 30 minutes. *6 servings*

Sausage Cocktail Balls

Mix 1 pound **TENNESSEE PRIDE® Hot Country Sausage** and 1 pound **TENNESSEE PRIDE® Mild Country Sausage**. Form sausage into bite-size balls. Set aside. Mix 1 cup currant jelly or apple jelly with ½ cup prepared mustard. Heat mixture until jelly is almost dissolved. Add sausage balls and simmer for 30 minutes. Serve with toothpicks.

Hot Beef 'n Frank Tidbits*

1 pound ground lean beef
1 egg, lightly beaten
¼ cup soft bread crumbs
3 tablespoons **LEA & PERRINS** Worcestershire Sauce, divided
2 tablespoons catsup, divided
¼ teaspoon salt
1/16 teaspoon **TABASCO®** Sauce
2 tablespoons oil
½ cup red currant jelly
1 jar (6 oz.) cocktail frankfurters, drained

In a mixing bowl combine beef, egg, bread crumbs, 1 tablespoon each of the **LEA & PERRINS** and catsup, salt and **TABASCO®**. Mix well, but do not overmix. Shape into 1-inch balls. In a large skillet heat oil. Add meatballs and brown well on all sides. Remove and drain on paper towels. Discard fat from skillet. In same skillet combine jelly, remaining 2 tablespoons **LEA & PERRINS** and 1 tablespoon catsup. Heat and stir until jelly melts. Add meatballs and frankfurters. Cover and cook 10 minutes, stirring occasionally, until mixture bubbles.

Yield: about 35 meatballs and 12 frankfurters

*May be prepared in advance of serving.

Tangy Sausage Bits

1 lb. ARMOUR® STAR German Brand Sausage
1 12-oz. can beer
1 tablespoon prepared mustard

Dip:
2 tablespoons dry mustard
2 tablespoons hot water
2 tablespoons dairy sour cream
1 tablespoon vinegar
¼ teaspoon ginger

Simmer sausage in beer and mustard for 15 minutes; drain. Cut sausage in 1-inch pieces.

Dip: Combine dry mustard, water, sour cream, vinegar and ginger. Serve as a dip for sausage pieces. *24 appetizers*

Sausages in Rum

2 tablespoons butter
1 pound small link sausages
½ cup brown sugar
½ cup soy sauce
½ cup **JACQUIN'S Rum**
Pepper

Melt the butter in a pan or chafing dish. Add sausages and cook briskly until brown. Pour off all but 2 tablespoons of fat. Add brown sugar, soy sauce and pepper to taste. Simmer 5 minutes on low heat. Warm the **JACQUIN'S Rum**, ignite it and pour over sausages. Serve with toothpicks for spearing. Count 3 or 4 sausages for each guest.

Little Links in Sauce

Add **OSCAR MAYER Brand Little Wieners** or **Little Smokies Sausage** to one of the sauces below. Prepare sauce; add little links and heat about 5 minutes longer, stirring occasionally. Serve in chafing dish with picks.

Four packages make 64 appetizers

Little Rubies

Heat together 1 can (21 oz.) cherry pie filling and ¼ cup rosé wine.

Orange Nutmeg

Combine ½ cup sugar with 2 tablespoons cornstarch and ½ teaspoon nutmeg. Stir in 1¼ cups orange juice. Cook over medium heat, stirring constantly until mixture boils and is thickened. Stir in 1 can (11 oz.) mandarin orange segments, drained.

Barbecue

Heat 1 bottle (18 oz.) barbecue sauce.

Currant

Heat 2 jars (10 oz. each) currant jelly.

Saucy Bourbon Bites

> 1 cup firmly-packed **COLONIAL® Light Golden Brown Sugar**
> 1 cup bourbon
> 1 cup chili sauce
> 2 pounds frankfurters, cut into bite-size pieces

Preheat oven to 325°. In 2-quart casserole, combine sugar, bourbon and chili sauce; stir in frankfurters. Bake, uncovered, 1½ hours, stirring once during baking. (OR, simmer in large skillet, on top of range, 30 to 45 minutes; stir occasionally.) Serve hot in chafing dish. Refrigerate leftovers.

Makes 8 dozen appetizers

Tip: Flavor is improved if made a day ahead; reheat before serving.

Appetizer Ham Chunks

> ¾ cup chili sauce
> ½ cup grape jelly
> 1 tablespoon lemon juice
> **WILSON® Ham**

Combine chili sauce, grape jelly and lemon juice in a small saucepan. Cook over medium heat, stirring frequently, until mixture comes to a boil. Reduce heat and simmer 5 minutes. Make sure all jelly is combined with chili sauce. Cut 48 cubes about ¾″ each from the ham. Serve with toothpicks for dipping ham in sauce.

Makes 48 appetizer servings

Scarlett O'Hara Ham Tidbits

> 1 slice ½″ thick center-cut boiled or baked ham (about 1 lb.)
> ½ stick butter or margarine
> ¾ cup **OCEAN SPRAY Cranberry Juice Cocktail**
> ½ cup crushed unsweetened pineapple
> Juice of 1 lime
> 1 Tbsp. soy sauce
> 2 Tbsp. orange marmalade
> 2 Tbsp. dark brown sugar
> ½ cup **SOUTHERN COMFORT®**

Cube ham; sauté in butter, stirring constantly, until slightly brown. Add all ingredients except **SOUTHERN COMFORT®**. Cook over low heat, stirring occasionally, until liquid is reduced to heavy syrup consistency. Add 2 oz. **SOUTHERN COMFORT®**; stir 1 minute. Add remaining **SOUTHERN COMFORT®**. Stand back and ignite. Stir until flames subside and the mixture thickens. Serve on toothpicks.

Makes 20 to 25 tidbit pieces

Chinese Barbecued Pork
(Char Siu)

> ½ cup **KIKKOMAN Soy Sauce**
> ⅓ cup honey
> ¼ cup sherry
> 1 teaspoon red food coloring
> ¼ teaspoon garlic powder
> ¼ teaspoon ground ginger
> 2 pounds boneless pork loin roast (boned, rolled and tied)
> **Mustard-Soy Sauce***
> **Toasted sesame seed**

Blend together soy sauce, honey, sherry, red food coloring, garlic and ginger. Unroll pork roast; cut lengthwise into 3 equal strips. Place in large shallow pan; add marinade and turn over several times to coat thoroughly. Cover and refrigerate 12 to 24 hours, turning over occasionally. Remove pork and lay on rack placed over pan of water. Insert meat thermometer into thickest part of 1 strip. Roast in 325°F. oven 30 minutes. Turn strips over and roast about 20 minutes longer, or until meat thermometer registers 165°. Remove from rack and cool at room temperature. At serving time, cut each strip into thin slices. Dip each slice of Chinese Barbecued Pork into Mustard-Soy Sauce, then toasted sesame seed.

Makes about 4 dozen appetizers

(Continued)

6

*Mustard-Soy Sauce

Blend 2 tablespoons dry mustard with water to make a smooth paste. Thin with **KIKKOMAN Soy Sauce** to dipping consistency.

Barbequed Spareribs

2 pounds pork spareribs
1 cup apple juice
1 tablespoon soy sauce
2 tablespoons hoisin sauce or catsup
1 tablespoon honey
1 packet **SWEET 'N LOW®**

In large saucepan of boiling water, simmer ribs about 5 minutes to remove excess fat. Drain. In shallow baking dish, combine remaining ingredients. Add ribs and marinate 2 to 3 hours. Preheat oven to 350°F. Bake, uncovered, 45 minutes. Increase temperature to 450°F and continue baking 5 to 10 minutes, or until very tender.   *24 servings*

Calories: 80 per serving (1 rib)

Oriental Sausage Tidbits

1 pound **WILSON®** Smoked Sausage
2 (8 oz.) cans water chestnuts, drained
1 (11 oz.) can drained mandarin oranges (optional)
2 tablespoons soy sauce
¼ cup ketsup
2 tablespoons brown sugar
Dash garlic powder
¼ teaspoon ground ginger
36-40 bamboo skewers or wooden picks

Slice sausage in ½" pieces. Cut large water chestnuts in half, leaving smaller ones whole to make about 36. With wooden pick or skewer, spear through center of one sausage, water chestnut and orange segment. Combine remaining ingredients. Brush mixture on tidbits. Broil until sausage is heated, 2-3 minutes, and glazed. Turn once.   *Makes approximately 36*

Bonnie Beef Bites

1½ pounds top round steak, cut ¾ inch thick
¼ cup **JOHNNIE WALKER RED** Scotch
1 teaspoon grated fresh ginger root
1 clove garlic, crushed
¼ cup soy sauce
¼ cup oil
½ teaspoon sugar
½ cup toasted sesame seeds

Slice meat diagonally, as for London Broil, in very thin strips. Weave a bamboo skewer through each strip. Combine remaining

ingredients, except sesame seeds, and pour over skewers. Let stand about 2 hours, turning once. Remove skewers from marinade, broil about 1 minute each side, so that meat remains pink. Dip skewers in toasted sesame seeds before serving.
12 to 15 appetizer servings

Kabobs

HILLSHIRE FARM® Smoked Sausage
Kabob Ingredients:
Chunked green pepper
Water chestnuts
Onion wedges or pearl onions
Cherry tomatoes
Mushrooms
Sliced zucchini
Pineapple chunks
Basting Sauces:
Teriyaki sauce
Barbecue sauce
Orange marmalade spiced with dry mustard

Cut sausage into bite-sized pieces. Using small skewers, alternate sausage pieces with any of the kabob ingredients. Marinate and/or baste with one of the sauces. Broil or grill, turning skewers over and basting as the meat browns.

MICROWAVE METHOD:
Prepare as above, using wooden skewers. Place kabobs on a microwave safe roasting rack. If using 1 pound of sausage plus ingredients, microwave, uncovered, HIGH, 4-6 minutes or until hot, turning skewers over and basting once.

Tabasco® Barbecued Spareribs

3 pounds spareribs
Salt
1 tablespoon butter or margarine
1 medium onion, chopped
1 can (8 ounces) tomato sauce
1 tablespoon vinegar
1 tablespoon lemon juice
2 tablespoons brown sugar
1 teaspoon dry mustard
½ teaspoon **TABASCO®** Pepper Sauce
1 bay leaf
1 clove garlic
¼ cup water

Have sparerib rack cut into 3 lengthwise strips. Cut strips into individual ribs for out-of-hand eating. Place meat side up in shallow baking pan. Sprinkle with salt. Bake in 450°F. oven 30 minutes. Drain off fat.

Combine remaining ingredients in saucepan. Bring sauce to a boil; remove from heat. Brush spareribs with part of the sauce. Reduce oven temperature to 350° F. Bake spareribs 30 minutes. Turn ribs, brush with sauce and bake 30 minutes longer, brushing frequently with remaining sauce.

Yield: 24 appetizer servings

Glazed Mini Ribs

6 pounds or 2 racks of spareribs
Water
1 jar (8.5-oz.) **SMUCKER'S Low Sugar Blackberry Spread**
¾ cup catsup
¼ cup bottled steak sauce
1 teaspoon dry mustard
1 clove garlic, minced

Have the butcher cut the ribs crosswise through the bones to form 2½-to-3-inch wide strips. Boil 3-4 quarts of water in large stockpot. Place the ribs in pot, making sure there is enough water to cover. Reduce heat to simmer; cover; simmer ribs over low heat until fork tender, about 25 minutes. Drain. (Ribs can be cooked ahead and refrigerated.) Just before serving, line two jelly-roll pans or broiler pans with foil. Cut strips of ribs into individual ribs. Arrange in a single layer in pans. Broil, 1 pan at a time, about 4 inches from heat source for 10 minutes, turning once.

Meanwhile, in a small saucepan, combine remaining ingredients for the glaze. Heat to boiling; simmer over low heat for 10 minutes. Brush ribs with glaze and continue to broil, turning and basting frequently, for about 5 more minutes.

Serve ribs in a chafing dish over a heat source or place on a plate and keep warm on an electric hot tray.

Makes about 12 appetizer servings

Chinese Egg Rolls

Filling:
1 lb. ground beef
¼ cup butter
4 cups finely shredded cabbage, partially cooked
½ cup finely chopped green onion
1½ cups finely diced celery
1 can (1 lb.) **LA CHOY® Fancy Bean Sprouts**, drained
¼ cup **LA CHOY® Soy Sauce**
1 teaspoon salt
2 tablespoons sugar
½ teaspoon monosodium glutamate desirable

Brown beef lightly in butter. Add vegetables and seasonings and cook about 5 minutes. Drain and cool. Prepare Egg Roll batter.

Batter:
2 cups sifted flour
2 tablespoons cornstarch
1 teaspoon salt
1 egg, beaten
1 teaspoon sugar
2 cups water
Peanut Oil

To the sifted dry ingredients add egg and sugar. Gradually beat in water until a smooth thin batter is formed. Grease a 6-inch skillet lightly with oil. Pour about 4 tablespoons of batter into center of pan. Tilt pan to spread batter over entire surface. Cook over low heat until edges pull away from sides; gently turn pancake with fingers and cook other side. Remove from pan and cool. Place a heaping tablespoon of filling in center of each pancake. Spread to within ½ inch of edge. Roll, folding in sides and seal with a mixture of 1 tablespoon flour and 2 tablespoons water. Fry egg rolls in deep hot fat (360°) until golden brown.

Chinese Egg Rolls should be served hot as an appetizer or side dish with mustard sauce which can be prepared simply by mixing dry mustard powder with hot water to the desired strength.

Yield: 20 egg rolls

Wheat Germ Egg Rolls

1 cup bean sprouts, coarsely chopped
¾ cup **KRETSCHMER Regular Wheat Germ**
½ cup grated carrot
½ cup green onion, cut into 1½-inch pieces
½ cup minced water chestnuts
3 Tbsp. soy sauce
2 Tbsp. dry sherry
1 tsp. grated ginger root
12 egg roll skins
1 tsp. cornstarch
3 Tbsp. water
Oil for frying

Combine all ingredients *except* egg roll skins, cornstarch, water and oil for frying. Mix well. Wrap skins in damp paper toweling, taking out one at a time. Place ¼ cup filling on each skin. Cover half the skin, leaving a narrow border along bottom and side edges. Fold narrow edge up over filling. Fold in side edges. Roll to within ½ inch of top edge. Brush top edge with cornstarch mixed with water. Seal well. Cover with damp paper toweling. Heat oil (about 3 inches deep) to 350°. Fry egg rolls, a few at a time, about 3 minutes until golden. Drain well. Cut each roll diagonally into 3 pieces. Serve hot.

Makes 3 dozen appetizers

Egg Rolls Azteca®

Heat in Skillet:
    1 Tbsp. oil
Sauté:
    1 medium onion, sliced very thin
Add and Cook 2 Minutes:
    2 cups chopped bok choy
Cook about 1 minute. Stir in:
    2 cups cooked ham, chicken or pork, cut into ¼″ cubes
    1 14 oz. can bean sprouts
    2 Tbsp. soy sauce
    ½ tsp. sugar
Blend:
    1 Tbsp. cornstarch
    2 Tbsp. water or chicken broth
Add to meat mixture, stirring until thickened. Soften:
    10 **AZTECA® Flour Tortillas**

Place 2-3 Tbsp. meat on one side of tortillas, near edge. Fold in sides and roll. Secure with a toothpick. Dip in batter* and deep fat fry.

*Batter

¼ cup flour
1 egg
1 Tbsp. vegetable oil
¼ cup water

Thoroughly mix all ingredients together.

Pork Sausage Wontons

1 pkg. (1 lb.) **OSCAR MAYER Ground Pork Sausage**
1 can (8 oz.) water chestnuts, drained, finely chopped
2 green onions, finely chopped
30 wonton skins, 3½-inch square
Peanut or vegetable oil for frying

In skillet cook sausage over medium heat about 12 min., stirring and separating sausage as it cooks; drain on absorbent paper. Combine sausage, water chestnuts and onion. Place 1 Tbsp. sausage mixture on center of wonton skin. Moisten corners of wonton skin with water and fold up over sausage mixture like an envelope. Pinch to seal.* Heat at least 1-inch oil in heavy skillet, wok or deep fat fryer to 375°F. Fry wontons until golden brown, turning once. Drain on absorbent paper. Serve with sweet and sour sauce and Chinese hot mustard. *Makes 30*

*Wontons and skins should be covered with moist towel when they are not being handled; they have a tendency to dry out and become brittle.

Irish Mist® *Liqueur*

Bantry Bay Shrimp Toast

1 package (8 oz.) cream cheese, softened
1 can (4½ oz.) shrimp, rinsed and drained
¼ cup mayonnaise
2 tablespoons **IRISH MIST®** liqueur
1 tablespoon lemon juice
1 tablespoon finely minced parsley
Sliced party rye bread, toasted

In medium bowl, combine all ingredients except toast. Spread on toast. Broil until lightly browned and puffed. Garnish with shrimp. Also delicious cold. *Makes 25*

Teriyaki Meat Sticks

½ cup **KIKKOMAN Soy Sauce**
¼ cup chopped green onions and tops
2 tablespoons sugar
1 tablespoon vegetable oil
1½ teaspoons cornstarch
1 clove garlic, crushed
¼ teaspoon ground ginger *or* 1 teaspoon grated fresh
    ginger root
2½ pounds beef sirloin steak, boned and trimmed of fat

Blend soy sauce, green onions, sugar, oil, cornstarch, garlic and ginger in saucepan. Simmer, stirring constantly, until thickened, about 1 minute. Cool, cover & keep at room temperature.

Slice meat into ⅛-inch thick strips about 4 inches long and 1 inch wide. Thread bamboo or metal skewers each with 1 strip of meat. Wrap and refrigerate; when ready to serve, brush skewered meat on both sides with sauce. Arrange on serving tray. Let guests cook Meat Sticks on charcoal hibachi to desired doneness.
Makes about 5 dozen

THE CHRISTIAN BROTHERS®

Ginger Pork Balls in Sherry-Orange Sauce

1 large slice white bread, crumbled (about 1 cup crumbs)
¼ cup **THE CHRISTIAN BROTHERS®** Golden
    Sherry
1½ pounds lean ground pork
½ cup minced water chestnuts
2 tablespoons soy sauce
1 egg yolk
2 teaspoons ground ginger
1 large clove garlic, crushed
Sherry-Orange Sauce*

In large bowl combine bread and sherry; set aside 10 minutes. Add remaining ingredients except Sherry-Orange Sauce. Mix to blend thoroughly. Cover and chill at least 30 minutes. Form into 1-inch balls. Place slightly apart on baking sheet. Bake in 400 degree oven about 20 minutes until cooked through and lightly browned.

Meanwhile prepare Sherry-Orange Sauce. Add drained pork balls to sauce. Cook over medium heat until hot through, stirring gently. Remove from heat; gently stir in orange segments (reserved in Sherry-Orange Sauce recipe). Serve hot with cocktail picks for spearing. *Makes about 5 dozen*

*Sherry-Orange Sauce

2 cans (11 ounces *each*) mandarin orange segments
¾ cup chicken broth or bouillon
⅓ cup **THE CHRISTIAN BROTHERS®** Golden
    Sherry
2 tablespoons *each* cornstarch and soy sauce

Drain liquid from orange segments into 2-cup measure; reserve segments. Add broth to orange liquid to make 2 cups. Pour into 2-quart saucepan. Mix sherry, cornstarch and soy sauce; add to saucepan. Cook and stir over medium heat until smooth and thickened. Simmer 1 minute.

First Prize winner **THE CHRISTIAN BROTHERS®** contest

THE ORIGINAL WORCESTERSHIRE

Chicken Livers Hong Kong
(Low Calorie)

1 pound (about 12) chicken livers
1 can (8 oz.) water chestnuts, drained and halved
2 tablespoons **LEA & PERRINS** Worcestershire Sauce
1 tablespoon dry sherry
1 tablespoon soy sauce
1 teaspoon garlic powder
½ teaspoon salt
¼ teaspoon ground ginger

Cut chicken livers in half; place in a medium bowl. Stir in remaining ingredients. Cover and refrigerate for 1 hour. On wooden picks skewer a piece of liver and a water chestnut half. Place on a rack in a broiler pan. Broil under a preheated hot broiler until cooked as desired, about 2 minutes on each side. *About 2 dozen*

Calorie Count: about 58 calories per hors d'oeuvre

THE CHRISTIAN BROTHERS®
Rumaki

¾ lb. chicken livers
Canned water chestnuts
1 Tbsp. soy sauce
1 cup THE CHRISTIAN BROTHERS® Ruby Port
Bacon slices, cut in half

Cut livers into bite-size pieces; cut water chestnuts in half. Marinate for one hour or more in combined soy sauce and wine. Wrap bacon around liver and water chestnut; secure with wooden toothpick. Broil slowly until crisp. May be assembled ahead of time.
20-24 appetizers

ReaLemon® Rumaki

¼ cup REALEMON® Lemon Juice from Concentrate
¼ cup soy sauce
¼ cup vegetable oil
3 tablespoons catsup
2 cloves garlic, finely chopped
½ teaspoon pepper
12 chicken livers (about ½ pound)
8 water chestnuts
12 slices bacon, cut in half crosswise
Brown sugar

In medium bowl, combine REALEMON®, soy sauce, oil, catsup, garlic and pepper; set aside. Cut each chicken liver in half; cut each water chestnut into 3 pieces. Place in sauce; marinate in refrigerator 4 hours. Drain. Preheat oven to 450°. Wrap 1 piece of chicken liver and 1 piece of water chestnut in each bacon piece. Secure with toothpick; roll in brown sugar.

Place on rack in aluminum foil-lined shallow baking dish; bake 10 minutes. Turn; continue baking 15 minutes or until bacon is crisp. Serve hot. Refrigerate leftovers.   *Makes 24 appetizers*

SUN WORLD®
New Year's Date Rumaki

2 dozen SUN WORLD® Pitted Dates
Soy sauce
1 dozen water chestnuts
12 slices bacon

Marinate dates in soy sauce for 1-2 hours. Wrap one date and ½ water chestnut in half a bacon slice. Fasten with wooden pick. Broil until bacon is done. Serve hot as appetizers.

Coco Rumaki

½ pound liver (chicken, calf or baby steer)
¼ cup COCO CASA™ Cream of Coconut
½ pound bacon

Cut liver into bite-size pieces. Coat with cream of coconut. Cut bacon slices into thirds. Wrap each piece of liver with bacon and spear with a toothpick. Broil until crisp on both sides.

Turkey Rumaki

36 half inch chunks roast BUTTERBALL® Turkey
18 slices SWIFT PREMIUM® Bacon, cut in halves crosswise
36 slices water chestnuts
½ cup soy sauce
¼ cup packed brown sugar
¼ cup sherry or dry white wine
¼ teaspoon ground ginger
¼ teaspoon garlic powder

Partially cook bacon. Drain. Top each chunk of turkey with a slice of water chestnut, wrap with a half slice of bacon and secure with a wooden pick. Combine remaining ingredients. Marinate appetizers in sauce for several hours, turning occasionally. Place appetizers on rack in shallow pan and broil 4 to 5 minutes. Serve hot.
Yield: 36 appetizers

MICROWAVE METHOD:
Arrange 10 appetizers at a time in a circle on paper towel lined plate. Cover with paper towel. Microwave on HIGH 1 to 2 minutes or until bacon is crisp.

Chicken Kebobs
(Yakitori)

2½ to 3 pounds chicken breasts, whole or halves
1 pound chicken livers
1 bunch green onions
1 cup KIKKOMAN Soy Sauce
¼ cup sugar
1 tablespoon vegetable oil
2 cloves garlic, crushed
¾ teaspoon ground ginger

Remove skins and bones from chicken breasts, keeping meat in one piece; cut into 1-inch lengths. Thread bamboo skewers each with a chicken piece, a green onion piece (spear through the side), and a chicken liver piece. Combine soy sauce, sugar, oil, garlic and ginger. Place kebobs in large shallow baking pan; pour sauce over. Brush each kebob thoroughly with sauce. Marinate kebobs about 1 hour and remove; reserve marinade. Broil kebobs 5 inches below preheated broiler 3 minutes on each side, brushing with marinade after turning.   *Makes about 4 dozen*

Peanut Chicken Pick-Me-Ups
(Low Sodium)

2½ cups ground cooked chicken
½ cup grated carrots
½ cup minced fresh parsley
½ cup finely chopped onion
¾ cup low-sodium mayonnaise
1½ cups ground PLANTERS® Dry Roasted Unsalted Peanuts
¼ cup FLEISCHMANN'S® Unsalted Margarine, melted

Toss together chicken, carrots, parsley and onion. Add mayonnaise; mix well. Roll into 1-inch balls. Roll each ball in **PLANTERS® Dry Roasted Unsalted Peanuts**. Dip one side of ball in **FLEISCHMANN'S® Unsalted Margarine** and place on ungreased baking sheets, margarine side up.

Bake at 400°F. for 15 minutes, or until golden. Cool 5 minutes before serving. *Makes 36 1-inch pieces*

Calories: 95 per piece
Sodium: 8 mg per piece

Appetizer Chicken Mole

1 cup chicken broth
1 medium tomato, peeled
1 slice white bread
3 tablespoons **PLANTERS® Slivered Almonds**
3 tablespoons unsifted flour
2 tablespoons dark seedless raisins
1 tablespoon chopped onion
1 small clove garlic
⅛ teaspoon ground cinnamon
Dash red pepper sauce
Dash ground black pepper
Dash salt
¼ cup **DROSTE® Bittersweet Chocolate Liqueur**
3 whole cooked chicken breasts, skinned, boned and cut into 1-inch cubes
Tortilla chips

In a blender or food processor combine chicken broth, tomato, bread, **PLANTERS® Slivered Almonds**, flour, raisins, onions, garlic, cinnamon, red pepper sauce, black pepper and salt; process until smooth. Pour into a medium saucepan. Cook over medium heat, stirring occasionally until thick and very hot. Stir in **DROSTE® Bittersweet Chocolate Liqueur**; mix in chicken cubes. Continue cooking 15 to 17 minutes until sauce is very thick and chicken is well heated. Serve hot with tortilla chips. Garnish as desired. *Makes 8 to 10 Appetizer Servings*

Chicken Wing Umbrellas With Sherry

6 broiler-fryer chicken wings
¼ cup **KARO® Light Corn Syrup**
2 tablespoons soy sauce
1 tablespoon dry sherry
¼ teaspoon ground ginger (or 2 teaspoons fresh chopped ginger)

Separate wings into three pieces at joints. (Save wing tips for use in making chicken broth.) On remaining two sections loosen meat from joint with a sharp knife. Slide knife down bone to loosen entire surface leaving opposite joint end intact. Push meat down over intact end to form a ball. On section with two bones twist out smaller bone.

In 1-quart saucepan stir together corn syrup, soy sauce, sherry and ginger. Stirring occasionally bring to boil over medium heat

and boil 1 minute. Cool slightly; pour over drumsticks. Cover; refrigerate 6 hours or overnight.

Stand drumsticks in 9 x 5 x 3-inch loaf pan. Bake in 375°F oven basting occasionally, 35 minutes or until tender.

Makes 12 appetizers

MICROWAVE METHOD:
Prepare drumsticks as directed. In microproof cup stir together corn syrup, soy sauce, sherry and ginger. Microwave with full power 1 to 2 minutes. Cool slightly, pour over drumsticks. Cover; refrigerate 6 hours or overnight. On microproof plate arrange drumsticks spoke fashion with meat toward outside. Cover with waxed paper and microwave with full power 5 minutes. Brush with marinade. Uncover and microwave 3 to 4 minutes longer or until tender. To reheat drumsticks: Microwave with full power uncovered 1 to 2 minutes.

Hickory-Barbecued Chicken Wings a la Perrins

1 can (8 oz.) tomato sauce
2 tablespoons brown sugar
2 tablespoons **LEA & PERRINS Worcestershire Sauce**
2 tablespoons lemon juice
1 tablespoon onion powder
1½ teaspoons cornstarch
1½ teaspoons hickory smoked salt
3 pounds chicken wings, cut at the joint
Oil
Salt

To prepare barbecue sauce combine in a small saucepan tomato sauce, brown sugar, **LEA & PERRINS**, lemon juice, onion powder, cornstarch, and hickory smoked salt; blend well. Cook and stir until thickened, about 4 to 5 minutes; set aside.

Lightly brush chicken wings with oil; sprinkle lightly with salt. Arrange on a rack in a broiler pan. Place under a preheated moderate broiler (350 F.); broil about 10 to 12 minutes, turning once. Brush barbecue sauce over chicken wings; broil until chicken is tender, about 8 to 10 minutes longer, turning and brushing frequently with the sauce. Serve immediately, or freeze in a single layer on a shallow pan, covered with freezer wrap. Just before serving, unwrap and place in a preheated hot oven (400 F.) for 10 minutes, or until hot. *About 32 hors d'oeuvres*

Menehune Chicken

24 chicken wings
1 cup **KIKKOMAN Soy Sauce**
¾ cup finely chopped green onions & tops
⅓ cup sugar
4 teaspoons vegetable oil
1 clove garlic, crushed
1½ teaspoons ground ginger *or* 1 tablespoon grated fresh ginger root

(Continued)

11

(Continued)

Disjoint chicken wings; discard tips. Blend soy sauce, green onions, sugar, oil, garlic and ginger in large mixing bowl. Add chicken pieces; cover and marinate 30 minutes. Remove chicken; reserve marinade. Place chicken, side by side, in shallow baking pan, skin side down. Bake, uncovered in 350°F. oven 15 minutes. Turn pieces; baste with marinade, and bake 15 minutes longer.

Makes about 4 dozen appetizers

Teriyaki Tidbits

14 COOKIN' GOOD™ Chicken Wings (about 3 lbs.)

Marinade:
1 cup teriyaki sauce
½ cup molasses
½ cup lemon or lime juice
¼ cup honey
1 teaspoon of garlic powder or 1 clove fresh garlic crushed
¼ cup instant onions minced
1 cup vegetable oil
1 cup white wine
1 teaspoon paprika
Dipping sauce*

Disjoint wings, reserve tips for stock. In a large glass bowl, combine marinade ingredients. Add wing pieces and marinate at least four hours (preferably overnight).

CONVENTIONAL OVEN METHOD:
Preheat oven to 400 degrees. Drain marinade and reserve for basting and sauce recipe. Place wing pieces in a single layer in a shallow baking dish. Roast 35-45 minutes, basting often with marinade, until crisp and brown.

MICROWAVE METHOD:
Same as above except use a microwave baking dish. Microwave 12-15 minutes, full power, 650 watts. Baste and stir pieces often. Crisp under browning unit or conventional broiler.

*Dipping Sauce

   2 teaspoons of cornstarch
   1 cup of Marinade

Blend marinade and cornstarch together in a saucepan (without heat). Stirring constantly, bring the mixture to a boil over a medium heat until thick and bubbly. Serve this sauce with the Teriyaki Tidbits.

Simple Soy Wings

1 pkg. HOLLY FARMS® Wings
¼ cup cooking oil
3 Tbsp. soy sauce

Preheat oven to 350°F. Place wings in shallow baking dish. In a bowl, mix soy sauce and oil and brush on chicken. Bake uncovered, basting occasionally, for approximately 1 hour or until tender.

Zing Wings

2½ pounds chicken wings
6 tablespoons DURKEE RedHot! Sauce
¼ cup butter or margarine, melted

Split chicken wings at each joint and discard tips; pat dry. Deep fry at 400° (high) for 12 minutes or until crispy. Remove and drain well. (Can also be baked on a rack in a 400° oven for 25 minutes.) Combine hot sauce and butter. Dip chicken wings in sauce.

Makes 6 to 8 appetizer servings

Scallops en Brochette

Merely thaw 1 lb. **HIGH LINER® Scallops**. Wrap each one with a bacon strip, secure with a toothpick and sprinkle with salt, pepper and lemon juice. Broil 6-8 inches from element for 6-8 minutes.

Irish Mist® *Liqueur*

Celtic Oysters Rockefeller

¼ cup each chopped shallots and celery
3 sprigs parsley
1 cup butter (or margarine), softened
1 medium clove garlic, chopped
¼ teaspoon each chervil and tarragon
½ teaspoon each salt and fennel
Freshly ground pepper to taste
Dash TABASCO® Sauce
2 slices bread, broken in pieces
¼ cup IRISH MIST® liqueur
1 cup chopped fresh spinach
24 oysters on the half shell, cleaned and separated from the shell
Rock salt

In blender, combine all ingredients except spinach and oysters. Blend, scraping sides, until mixture is smooth. Cover each oyster with spinach. Top with one rounded teaspoon of paste. Place oysters on bed of rock salt in large shallow baking pan or oven-proof platter. Bake in preheated 450°F. oven 10 minutes.

Makes 24

Mandarin Shrimp

½ lb. **ATALANTA Frozen Shrimp**, raw, shelled deveined
½ lb. Mandarin orange sections
¼ cup Scallions, ½" pieces
¼ cup Butter, melted

On Skewers, alternate shrimp, orange section, scallion and shrimp. Brush with butter and broil 4 minutes on each side.

Yield: 6 Servings

Shrimp With Sweet-Sour Sauce

2 pounds (21 to 25-count per pound) raw, unpeeled shrimp
1 cup cold water
⅔ cup cider vinegar
⅔ cup brown sugar, firmly packed
2 tablespoons cornstarch
2 tablespoons KIKKOMAN Soy Sauce
½ teaspoon TABASCO® Pepper Sauce

Peel shrimp, leaving tails on and devein. Cook in boiling salted water 5 minutes; drain and cool. Wrap and refrigerate. Combine water, vinegar, brown sugar, cornstarch and soy sauce in saucepan. Simmer, stirring constantly until thickened, about 1 minute. Cool, cover and store at room temperature.

Arrange shrimp in serving bowl. Add pepper sauce to sweet-sour sauce and bring to boil, stirring constantly. Pour sauce into serving bowl over candle warmer; serve with shrimp.
Makes about 4 dozen appetizers and 2 cups sauce

Shrimp Teriyaki

½ cup KIKKOMAN Soy Sauce
2 tablespoons sugar
2 tablespoons water
1 tablespoon vegetable oil
1½ teaspoons cornstarch
1 clove garlic, crushed
¼ teaspoon ground ginger *or* 1 teaspoon grated fresh ginger root
2 pounds (21 to 25-count per pound) raw shrimp, shelled and deveined

Blend soy sauce, sugar, water, oil, cornstarch, garlic and ginger in saucepan. Simmer, stirring constantly until thickened, about 1 minute. Cool. Coat shrimp in sauce; drain off excess. Place on rack of broiler pan. Broil 5 inches from heat 3 to 4 minutes on each side. Remove and cool slightly. Thread each shrimp on short bamboo skewer; arrange on serving tray. Warm shrimp over charcoal hibachi on buffet table.
Makes about 4 dozen appetizers

Mrs. Paul's

Seafood Hors d'Oeuvres

1 package (7 ounces) MRS. PAUL'S® French Fried Scallops or
1 package (6 ounces) MRS. PAUL'S® French Fried Shrimp
1 pound sliced bacon, partially cooked

Prepare MRS. PAUL'S® French Fried Scallops or French Fried Shrimp as directed on package. Wrap each scallop or shrimp with one slice of bacon. Secure with toothpick. Broil approximately 6-8 inches from heat source for about 1 minute on each side or until bacon is crisp. Watch closely so bacon will not burn.

Elegant Crab Meat Balls

2 cans (6 to 7 ounces each) crab meat
1 cup fresh bread crumbs
3 tablespoons HOLLAND HOUSE® Sherry Cooking Wine
1 tablespoon lemon juice
1 tablespoon grated onion
1 teaspoon dry mustard
½ teaspoon salt
Pepper to taste
Bacon slices (about 12), cut in halves

Drain and flake crab meat; combine with remaining ingredients except bacon; mix well. Shape into walnut-size balls. Wrap with bacon; secure with toothpicks. Broil under medium heat until bacon is crisp, about 10 minutes, turning to brown evenly. Garnish with parsley and lemon.
Makes about 2 dozen

Amaretto di Amore® Crab Canapés

1 package (6 oz.) frozen snow crab, thawed and drained
1 can (8 oz.) sliced water chestnuts, drained and finely chopped
1 package (3 oz.) cream cheese, softened
2 tablespoons chopped scallions
2 tablespoons AMARETTO DI AMORE® Liqueur
1 tablespoon minced fresh parsley
1 teaspoon Dijon mustard
Butter, softened
18 1-inch thick slices French bread

Combine crab, water chestnuts, cream cheese, scallions, AMARETTO DI AMORE® Liqueur, parsley and mustard.

Lightly butter one side of each slice of French bread. Place slices under broiler until lightly toasted. Turn slices over, butter and toast under broiler. Spread one side of each slice with crab mixture. Broil until hot and bubbling, about 2 to 3 minutes. Serve hot.
Makes 18 Canapés

Chile Cheese Bites
(Low Calorie)

1 can (6½ oz.) BUMBLE BEE® Chunk Light Tuna in Water
4 eggs, lightly beaten
1 cup lowfat cottage cheese
1 cup shredded Monterey Jack cheese
1 can (4 oz.) diced green chiles
¼ cup flour
½ teaspoon baking powder
¼ teaspoon salt

Drain tuna. Combine eggs, cheeses and green chiles. Mix together dry ingredients and add to egg mixture along with tuna. Blend together and pour into buttered 8-inch square baking dish. Bake in 350° F oven 35 to 40 minutes. Let set 5 minutes before cutting into bite-size squares.
Makes 36 appetizers

Calories: 37 per appetizer

BOOTH

Nor'east Nibbles

16 frozen **BOOTH Fish Sticks**
½ cup grated Parmesan cheese
2 tablespoons butter or margarine
Sea Sauce*

Preheat oven to 450°. Cut frozen fish sticks into thirds. Roll each piece in cheese. Melt butter in a baking pan, 15″ × 10″ × 1″. Place fish in pan. Bake 8 to 10 minutes. Turn carefully. Bake 8 to 10 minutes longer or until crisp and brown. Drain on absorbent paper. Serve with hot Sea Sauce.   *Makes 48 hors d'oeuvres*

*Sea Sauce

1 can (8 ounces) tomato sauce
¼ cup chili sauce
¼ teaspoon garlic powder
¼ teaspoon oregano
¼ teaspoon liquid hot pepper sauce
¼ teaspoon thyme
⅛ teaspoon sugar
Dash basil

Combine all ingredients. Simmer 10 to 12 minutes, stirring occasionally.   *Makes 1 cup sauce*

Sardine Spirals

2 cans **KING OSCAR Sardines**, drained
4 tsp. lemon juice
¾ tsp. prepared horseradish
Bread, sliced ¼″ thick
Melted butter
Grated Parmesan cheese

Mash sardines with lemon juice and horseradish. Trim crusts from bread. Spread mixture on bread slices. Roll bread up, cut in half crosswise, fasten with picks. Brush with melted butter, sprinkle with Parmesan. Place on shallow pan; toast quickly in hot oven (475°).

Tuna Chili con Queso

1 tablespoon butter or margarine
¼ cup chopped onion
1 can (1 pound) tomatoes, drained and cut up
1 bay leaf
2 tablespoons flour
¼ cup milk
1 can (4 ounces) green chilies, drained, seeded, and chopped
1 cup (4 ounces) shredded Monterey Jack or mild Cheddar cheese
1 can (6½ or 7 ounces) **STAR-KIST® Tuna**, drained
¼ teaspoon salt
Corn Chips

Melt butter in a medium saucepan. Sauté onion until tender. Add tomatoes and bay leaf. Simmer 5 minutes, stirring occasionally. Mix flour and milk to make a paste. Add to saucepan. Simmer 5 minutes. Remove bay leaf. Add green chilies and cheese. Stir until cheese melts. Stir in **STAR-KIST® Tuna** and salt. Keep warm and serve with corn chips.   *Yield: about 2½ cups*

Hot Mushroom Appetizer

½ cup butter
1 cup chopped onion
1½ lbs. small, whole mushrooms
½ cup minced parsley
1 cup beef gravy
1 bay leaf
½ cup **BÉNÉDICTINE** liqueur

Melt butter in a large skillet. Add onions and sauté until soft. Add mushrooms and toss over high heat until lightly sautéed. Add parsley, beef gravy, bay leaf, and **BÉNÉDICTINE**. Heat, stirring until mixture comes to a boil. Boil 3 minutes. Serve in a chafing dish as an appetizer or on toast as an individual first course.   *Serves 8*

Dunphy's Stuffed Mushrooms

18 medium mushrooms
2 tablespoons butter
¼ cup finely chopped onion
¼ cup **DUNPHY'S Cream Liqueur**
1 package (3 oz.) cream cheese, softened
1 cup fresh whole wheat bread crumbs
¼ cup minced fresh parsley
¼ cup grated Swiss cheese

Remove stems from mushrooms, reserving caps. Finely chop stems. Melt butter in a skillet over medium heat; sauté mushroom stems and onion until tender, about 2 to 3 minutes, stirring occasionally. Set aside.

Gradually beat **DUNPHY'S Cream Liqueur** into softened cream cheese. Blend in mushroom mixture, bread crumbs and parsley. Fill mushroom caps with stuffing and place in a greased 11″ × 7″ × ½″ baking pan. Sprinkle cheese evenly over mushrooms. Broil 4 to 5 minutes, or until cheese melts and is golden brown. Serve hot. Garnish if desired.   *Makes 18 Appetizers*

French's® Stuffed Mushrooms

30 large size fresh mushrooms (about 1 lb.)
Salt and **FRENCH'S® Pepper**
¼ cup minced green onions
¼ cup butter or margarine
¼ cup sherry
¼ cup water
¾ cup **FRENCH'S® Big Tate Mashed Potato Flakes**
⅓ cup grated Parmesan cheese
FRENCH'S® Paprika

Remove caps from mushrooms; arrange, hollow side up, in buttered shallow baking dish. Season with salt and pepper. Chop mushroom stems; cook, with onion, in the ¼ cup butter 4 to 5 minutes, until tender, stirring occasionally. Remove from heat; add sherry and water. Stir in potato flakes and cheese to make a stiff mixture. Place a generous spoonful in each mushroom cap; sprinkle with paprika. Bake in 375° oven 15 minutes, until hot. Serve as hors d'oeuvres.

MICROWAVE METHOD:
Mushrooms can be prepared and stuffed ahead of time. Refrigerate until serving time. Cover loosely with wax paper. Cook on HIGH 3 minutes; rotate pan ½ turn and cook 2 to 3 minutes, until piping hot.

Stuffed Mushrooms

1 pound medium mushrooms (about 18)
¼ cup butter or margarine, melted
¼ cup green onions, finely chopped
¼ cup water, white wine or sherry
1 cup **PEPPERIDGE FARM® Herb Seasoned Stuffing**

Wash mushrooms and remove stems. Dip caps in melted butter and place upside down in a shallow baking pan. Finely chop ¼ cup of the mushroom stems and sauté with green onions in remaining butter, adding more butter if necessary. Add water or wine. Lightly stir in stuffing. Spoon mixture into mushroom caps. Bake at 350°F. until hot, about 10 minutes.

Makes about 18 hors d'oeuvres

Sausage and Mushroom Appetizer

Remove the stems from fresh mushrooms and wash mushroom caps. Cut **SWIFT PREMIUM® BROWN 'N SERVE™ Sausage Links** into thirds. Place mushroom caps in a shallow pan or on a broiler rack, smooth side up. Brush each with melted butter. Broil about 5 inches from the heat source for 3 minutes. Turn and brush with melted butter. Place ⅓ sausage link in center of each mushroom cap. Broil 2 minutes. Insert a pick in each, making sure to secure sausage and mushroom. Serve hot.

Dorman's® White Caps

Stem medium mushrooms, fill caps with **DORMAN'S® Natural Swiss Cheese** or **Mozzarella**, shredded, and bake in preheated hot 400° F. oven until cheese just melts, about 5 minutes. Serve hot or at room temperature.

Stuffed Cabbage
(Low Calorie)

2 medium-size onions, cut in chunks
1 large head cabbage
2 pounds lean ground veal or beef
Freshly ground pepper to taste
1 teaspoon garlic powder
2 cups tomato juice, divided
4 packets **SWEET 'N LOW®**
2 tablespoons lemon juice

In large saucepan, cook onions and cabbage in boiling water about 5 minutes. Drain, leaving onions in saucepan and removing cabbage. Mix ground meat with pepper, garlic powder, and ½ cup tomato juice. Divide in 18 portions. Separate cabbage leaves and place a portion of meat on each. Roll up and fasten with toothpick. Place in saucepan with onions. Stir **SWEET 'N LOW®** and lemon juice into remaining tomato juice. Pour over all. Cover and gently simmer 1 hour, or until cabbage is tender and meat is cooked through.
18 servings

Calories: 110 per serving (1 cabbage roll)

Impromptu Fondue

1 16-oz. jar **CHEEZ WHIZ Pasteurized Process Cheese Spread**
½ cup **PARKAY Margarine**
French bread chunks

Heat process cheese spread and margarine over low heat in fondue pot or saucepan, stirring occasionally, until process cheese spread melts. Serve hot with bread.
2 cups

Italian Fondue

½ pound ground beef
1 can (15 oz.) tomato paste
1 tablespoon cornstarch
4 cups (1 lb.) **SARGENTO Shredded Natural Mozzarella**
1 small container (8 oz.) creamed cottage cheese
½ cup dry white wine
1 teaspoon salt
1½ teaspoons oregano
¼ teaspoon freshly ground pepper
1 loaf French or Italian bread cut in chunks with crust on each

In a small skillet brown ground beef. Stir in tomato paste and cornstarch; heat until warmed. Transfer to fondue pot; place over low heat. Stir in cheeses, a little at a time, until they begin to melt. Stir in wine and continue to stir until cheese is fully melted and wine is blended into mixture. Stir in seasonings. Keep over low heat. Dip bread chunks into mixture using a fondue fork.
Yield: 6 servings

Hunt's®
Chilies con Queso

½ lb. process American cheese, cut into ½-inch cubes
1 (6 oz.) can **HUNT'S® Tomato Paste**
1 cup water
1 (4-oz.) can diced green chilies
½ cup minced onion
¼ cup diced green pepper
2 tsp. lemon juice
¼ tsp. **TABASCO®**
Tortilla or corn chips

In a saucepan, melt cheese over low heat. Meanwhile, combine remaining ingredients *except* tortilla chips in a small bowl; stir into melted cheese. Serve in fondue pot or chafing dish with tortilla chips.
Makes 1 quart

Butter Buds®

Butter Buds® Cheese Fondue

½ cup low-fat milk
1 teaspoon cornstarch
½ packet (4 teaspoons) **BUTTER BUDS®**
1 tablespoon chopped fresh parsley
White pepper to taste
2 drops hot pepper sauce
⅛ teaspoon garlic powder
⅛ teaspoon marjoram
⅓ cup grated Swiss cheese
⅓ cup grated part-skim mozzarella cheese
¼ cup white wine
6 ounces (4 to 6 slices) Italian or French bread with hard crust, cut in 1-inch cubes

Combine milk and cornstarch in top of double boiler. Heat over boiling water. Add **BUTTER BUDS®**, parsley, pepper, hot pepper sauce, garlic powder, and marjoram. Blend thoroughly. Add cheeses, stirring constantly until melted. Add wine gradually and stir until smooth. Transfer to fondue pot and keep hot during service. Using fork, dip bread into fondue.   *¾ cup*

Calories: 235 per serving (about ⅓ cup). By using **BUTTER BUDS®** instead of butter in this recipe, you have saved 190 calories and 70 mg of cholesterol per serving.

Supreme Plum Fondue

2 jars (7¾ oz. each) **GERBER® Junior Plums With Tapioca**
2 tablespoons chopped onion
2 tablespoons brown sugar
2 tablespoons prepared mustard
1 teaspoon horseradish
1 teaspoon garlic salt
1 package hot dogs

Combine all ingredients except hot dogs in medium saucepan. Stir well. Begin cooking over low heat. Cut hot dogs into bite size slices. Add to mixture. Continue cooking over low heat until hot dog pieces are well flavored—about 30 minutes. Serve warm with toothpicks.   *Yield: Approximately 1¾ cups sauce*

VARIATION:

Various sausages may be used in place of hot dogs.

Danish Camembert Cheese Fondue

1 package (5¼ ounces) or 1 can (7 ounces) Danish Camembert, chilled
1 egg white, beaten just to blend
Very fine dry bread crumbs (about ¼ cup)
Dash salt
Dash paprika

Cut the half moon package of Danish Camembert into 8 wedges, or the can into half and each half into 6 wedges. Dip each wedge of cheese into the egg white then into the bread crumbs which have been combined with salt and paprika.

Arrange crumb-coated cheese on wax paper-lined tray and chill till time to fry. Or cook the coated but still cold cheese immediately. Heat cooking oil to 375 degrees in electric or butane beef fondue pot. If you're using an alcohol burner or canned heat, first heat the oil in a pan on your kitchen range and transfer to the fondue pot. Let guests spear a wedge of the coated Camembert on long-handled forks and fry in the deep hot fat about 1 minute. Drain briefly on paper towels then eat immediately.

Most Americans like this fried cheese as is. But it's a Danish custom to serve the cheese with red currant jelly. Or with thin toast or crisp crackers. Allow about 1 package (5¼ ounces) of Danish Camembert per person. The egg white and bread crumbs go slightly further.

Favorite recipe from the **Denmark Cheese Association**

Swiss Fondue

1 Tbsp. flour
1½ cups **VIRGINIA DARE White Cooking Wine**
Half clove garlic
¾ lb. grated Swiss Cheese
Dash of pepper
Loaf of French bread

Stir flour vigorously into about ¼ cup cold **VIRGINIA DARE White Cooking Wine**; then add to remainder of wine in a fondue cooker or double boiler which has been rubbed with a cut clove of garlic. Heat to just below boiling. Slowly add cheese, stirring constantly. Continue stirring to a smooth consistency and add pepper to taste. Using long handled forks, spear bite-size pieces of French bread and dip into the fondue coating the bread chunk completely. If the fondue becomes too thick through prolonged cooking, it may be thinned with the addition of a little more cooking wine.   *Yield: 4 servings*

BOLLA
Imported Wines

Cheese Fondue

1 clove garlic
¾ lb. Jarlsburg cheese, shredded
¾ lb. Gruyere cheese, shredded
1¼ cup **Soave BOLLA** wine
3 tablespoons kirsch
3 teaspoons cornstarch
Dash nutmeg
French bread

Rub heavy saucepan and fondue pot with a garlic clove which has been sliced in half. In small container mix kirsch, cornstarch and nutmeg. Set aside. Heat wine in saucepan until it begins to bubble. Add cheese gradually, stirring constantly. Keep heat moderately high, but don't bring quite to boil. When cheese is melted, add kirsch mixture to it. Transfer the fondue to a fondue pot over low heat. It will thicken as it sets.

Never make ahead of time. Serve with French bread cut into 1-inch cubes with the crust on one side, and fondue forks.

Argo®/Kingsford's® Cheese Fondue

1 clove garlic
1 cup sauterne wine
1 cup dry white wine
1½ pounds imported Swiss cheese, cubed
1 tablespoon **ARGO®/KINGSFORD'S® Corn Starch**
3 tablespoons Kirsch
⅛ teaspoon ground nutmeg
1 (12-inch) French bread cut into 1-inch cubes

In top of double boiler with simmering water touching bottom of pan place garlic and wine. Heat just until boiling. Remove garlic. Add cheese, ½ at a time, stirring until melted. In small bowl stir together corn starch, Kirsch and nutmeg until smooth. Add to cheese mixture. Cook, stirring frequently, 5 minutes or until mixture is thickened. At this point mixture may be kept over simmering water 1 hour. (Check bottom of double boiler occasionally and add water as needed.)

Mixture may be served from double boiler or transferred to fondue pot. To serve, let each person spear bread with fondue forks and dip into hot cheese mixture.

Makes 6 to 8 servings as appetizer

Minted Lamb Appetizers

¾ lb. ground lamb
2 Tbsp. shallots, chopped
2 Tbsp. parsley, chopped
1 to 2 tbsp. **ASPEN™** Liqueur
10 drops hot pepper sauce
¼ cup cream cheese
Filo dough sheets
Melted butter

Sauté lamb, shallots and parsley until lightly browned. Remove from heat. Add **ASPEN™** and pepper sauce to cream cheese; mix well. Add to meat mixture and blend. Cut filo sheets into 2 inch strips. Brush with melted butter. Place small amount of lamb mixture at one end of filo strip. Roll into triangles as you would the American flag. Brush top side with butter and place on cookie sheet. Bake at 350°F. until edges turn golden brown.

Yield: 35 to 40 appetizers

Note: May be frozen before baking for future use.

Panzarotti

2 tablespoons margarine
1 package (15⅜ oz.) **CHEF BOY-AR-DEE® Complete Cheese Pizza Mix**
1 egg yolk (reserve white)
½ cup hot water
Three Cheese Filling*

Cut margarine into Pizza Flour Mix with knife or pastry cutter. Combine egg yolk and hot water. Add to flour mixture. Mix, about 25 strokes. Cover and let rise in a warm place for five minutes. Turn dough out on well-floured board. Knead 50 times, until dough is smooth and satiny. Roll out ⅛ inch thick. Use coffee cup as pattern; cut around with sharp knife to make three or four inch dough circles. Spread one teaspoon of filling on half of dough. Fold in half. Seal with fork dipped in flour. Fry or bake. Serve with hot pizza sauce, from package. *Yields 12*

To Fry: Heat approximately one inch oil or fat (2 to 2½ cups) in a skillet over medium heat. Fry pies until golden brown, turning once. Drain on absorbent paper.

To Bake: Arrange on cookie sheet. Brush with reserved egg white. Bake at 425° for 10 minutes.

*Three Cheese Filling

¼ cup Ricotta cheese
1 egg
2 tablespoons chopped parsley
Dash of nutmeg
Canned grated cheese from Pizza Mix package
¼ cup chopped mozzarella cheese

Mix all ingredients.

Brie en Croûte

1 egg yolk
1 **PEPPERIDGE FARM® Frozen "Bake It Fresh" Puff Pastry Sheet**
2 small Brie or Camembert

Beat egg yolk with 1 tablespoon water. Thaw puff pastry 20 minutes, then unfold. Cut pastry sheet into 4 squares. Roll out 1 pastry square until it is approximately ½ inch larger than the circle of cheese. Place Brie in center of circle and trim edges leaving a ½ inch border. Brush border with egg mixture. Roll second square of pastry until it is large enough to fit over the cheese again allowing the ½ inch border. Place over the circle of cheese and press to seal. Repeat with remaining pastry and cheese. If desired, decorate with cutouts made from pastry scraps (heart-shapes, crescents, twists etc.) and apply with egg mixture.

Brush *top only* with egg and place on an ungreased cookie sheet in the middle of a preheated 375° oven. Bake for 20 minutes or until golden brown. Serve warm or at room temperature.

Makes 12 servings

Snack Turnovers

1 pkg. frozen pie crusts (or 2 homemade crusts)
Filling:
1 10¾ oz. can shrimp (or ½ cup shredded chicken or beef)
1 tsp. minced onion
3 Tbsp. soy oil mayonnaise
1 tsp. lemon juice
3 Tbsp. grated Cheddar (or other hard) cheese
Salt & pepper to taste

Soy oil for deep frying

Thaw pie crusts. Drain shrimp and mix with all other Filling ingredients. Flatten pie crusts out with the sticky side up. Cut circles out of crusts with a biscuit cutter. Put one teaspoon of filling on each circle and fold over to form turnovers. Pinch edges

(Continued)

together with a fork. Deep fry in soy oil (frying temperature 375°) for 3-5 minutes or until golden brown. Drain on paper towels or brown paper bags. Serve hot.

Note: Turnovers can be made ahead and frozen in an airtight container. Thaw and remove ice crystals before frying. If you wish to freeze them, substitute sour cream or plain yogurt for the mayonnaise in the filling.

Favorite recipe from the **American Soybean Association**

Crusty Creamy Havarti
(Indbagt Havarti)

1 (7 oz.) round Creamy Havarti
1 Tbsp. Dijon mustard
¼ cup chopped mixed fresh herbs, such as, basil, dill, fennel, chives, watercress and parsley
3 frozen patty shells, thawed, or ½ sheet frozen puff pastry
1 egg lightly beaten
Watercress for garnish

Spread top of cheese with mustard; then cover with mixed herbs, pressing into mustard. Set aside. On pastry cloth, arrange 3 patty shells close together in a triangle; moisten edges that touch with water and pinch together securely. Gently roll dough to a circle about 9 inches. With 9 inch plate for pattern, cut circle, reserving scraps. Put cheese in center of circle, herb-side down. Gather edges of pastry over cheese, moistening overlapping edges and pinching tightly. Place on greased foil on shallow baking sheet, seam side down. Brush all over with beaten egg. Roll scraps and cut circle or small decorative designs; arrange on top. Chill for 30 minutes. Brush again with egg. Cup foil closely around side of cheese. Bake in preheated 375°F oven 15 minutes. Brush again with egg. Bake 15 minutes more or until golden brown. Cool 30 minutes on rack. Garnish with watercress. Serve lukewarm in wedges.

Note: Other Danish Cheeses, in approximately 7 oz. pieces, such as Svenbo, Danbo, Fontina and Camembert can be substituted for the round Creamy Havarti in this recipe. To wrap other shapes of cheese in pastry, be sure that dough is rolled large enough to cover cheese loosely and completely.

Cheese Baked In Pastry makes an excellent hors d'oeuvre served with fresh fruit. The unbaked wrapped cheese can be frozen and baked at your convenience.

Favorite recipe from the **Denmark Cheese Association**

Shrimp Turnovers

2 tablespoons butter
¼ cup chopped scallions
2 cloves garlic, minced
⅛ teaspoon ground black pepper
1 pound raw shrimp, cleaned and finely chopped
¼ cup **Manto Liqueur** by **METAXA®**
1 tablespoon fine dry bread crumbs
5 sheets filo pastry (16" × 12")
PLANTERS® Peanut Oil

Melt butter in a large skillet over medium heat. Add scallions, garlic and pepper; sauté 1 to 2 minutes. Mix in shrimp and sauté until pink and liquid in skillet evaporates; stir occasionally. Remove from heat. Add **Manto Liqueur** by **METAXA®** and bread crumbs; toss lightly.

Cut each sheet of filo pastry into five 12-inch long strips. (Keep filo pastry strips covered with a damp cloth to prevent drying while shaping turnovers.) Place a rounded teaspoon of shrimp filling at end of each strip. Fold one corner of each strip over filling, bringing corner to opposite side of strip. Continue folding entire length of strip to encase filling in triangular shaped turnovers. Moisten edges of pastry triangles with water to seal.

Deep fry in **PLANTERS® Peanut Oil** that has been heated to 400° F. for 3 minutes, or until golden. Serve immediately. Garnish with scallion brushes if desired.   *Makes 25 turnovers*

Pepperidge Farm® Patty Shell Hors d'Oeuvres

- Roll each thawed **PEPPERIDGE FARM®** Patty Shell to ⅛ inch thickness. Cut with a sharp knife into diamonds, squares, triangles and long narrow strips. Bake at 400°F. for 10 to 15 minutes or until puffed and brown. Cool and then top with desired filling. Use deviled ham topped with red caviar, chicken spread topped with olive slices, liver spread topped with crumbled crisp bacon, tartar sauce spread topped with tiny shrimp, melted butter sprinkled with celery salt, garlic salt and onion salt. Or spoon on a little canned cherry pie filling, topped with whipped cream and slices of strawberries.

- Cut 2 inch squares of the ⅛ inch thick puff pastry and top with a whole mushroom (canned), or a whole olive, or a cube of Cheddar, or cooked shrimp, or a piece of chicken liver or cube of ham. Brush edge with egg and fold over into a triangle. Bake at 400°F. for 15 to 20 minutes or until puffed and brown. Serve hot.

Almond-Sausage Cheese Tarts

Pastry:
1 cup butter or margarine, softened
1 package (8 ounces) cream cheese, softened
1 tablespoon chopped chives
1 teaspoon salt
3 cups sifted all-purpose flour

In medium-size bowl cream butter, cream cheese, chives and salt. Work in flour with a fork or pastry blender. Divide dough in half; shape into balls, wrap in waxed paper and refrigerate one hour. Roll each ball on sheet of aluminum foil into 12 × 15-inch rectangle, about ⅛-inch thick. Cut pastry and foil together with scissors into 1½ × 3-inch rectangles. Moisten ends with water; pinch together; spread out slightly into canoe-shape. Prick pastry well with fork to keep its shape. Place on cookie sheet. Bake in 400 degree F. oven 12 to 15 minutes or until golden. Remove foil. Prepare Almond-Sausage Filling*.

FOOD PROCESSOR METHOD:
Place metal blade in processor bowl; add chilled butter (do not soften) and cream cheese (each cut into pieces); process until

blended. Remove cover and add chives, salt and flour; mix until well blended. Remove dough from bowl, wrap in waxed paper, chill one hour. Proceed as directed above. (Depending on your processor, it may be easiest to do in two batches.)

*Almond-Sausage Filling:
1½ pounds medium-spiced pork sausage
⅓ cup **BLUE DIAMOND® Whole Blanched Almonds**, finely chopped
½ cup sliced green onion
Salt, pepper and garlic powder
2 tablespoons hot mustard
1 egg

In large skillet, brown meat, almonds and onion; season with salt, pepper and garlic powder to taste; remove from heat. Beat together mustard and egg and stir into meat mixture. Spoon into baked pastries. Bake in 375 degree F. oven for 10 minutes. Serve warm or at room temperature. *Makes about 7 dozen*

Note: Baked pastries may be wrapped and frozen, unfilled, up to 2 weeks.

Mexican Tarts

1 cup dairy sour cream
2 tablespoons taco sauce
¼ cup chopped green pepper (Mushrooms or ripe olives could be substituted.)
¾ cup coarsely crushed tortilla chips
1 pound lean ground beef
½ cup **3 MINUTE BRAND® Quick Oats** or 1 packet **Regular Flavor HARVEST BRAND® Instant Oatmeal**
2 tablespoons taco seasoning mix
2 tablespoons cold water
1 cup (4 ounces) shredded Cheddar cheese

In small bowl mix sour cream, taco sauce, green pepper and tortilla chips; set aside. In large bowl mix beef, oats, taco seasoning mix and cold water. Press meat mixture into bottom and up sides of 1½-inch miniature muffin cups, forming a shell. Place a spoonful of sour cream mixture in each shell, mounding slightly. Sprinkle cheese atop tarts. Bake in a 425°F oven for 7 to 8 minutes. *Makes 30 tarts*

Note: To make a main-dish pie, substitute a 9-inch pie plate for the muffin cups. Bake in a 375°F oven about 45 minutes.
Makes 6 main dish servings

Piccolo Pizza Tarts

1 8-oz. container butterflake-type dinner rolls
¾ cup tomato sauce
1 cup mozzarella cheese, shredded
2 3½ oz. packages **HORMEL Sliced Pepperoni**
Small muffin tin, cups 1½″ × 1″

Heat oven to 375°. For each tart remove two layers from rolls. Flatten in hand and gently pull out to a 4″ circle. Ease into muffin cups. To each cup add 1 tsp. sauce, 2 pepperoni halves crisscrossed and 1 tsp. cheese. Top with two pepperoni halves, criss-

crossed. Bake for 18-20 minutes, until deep golden brown on tops and sides of tarts. Remove from oven. Let cool slightly in tins for 5-10 minutes. Serve warm.

Olive Tarts

½ cup soft butter or margarine
½ pound (2 cups) finely grated American cheese
1 cup sifted all-purpose flour
¼ teaspoon **TABASCO®**
½ teaspoon salt
1 teaspoon paprika
36 small stuffed olives

Cream butter and cheese. Stir in flour, **TABASCO®**, salt and paprika. Wrap 1 teaspoon of mixture around each olive, covering completely. Arrange on baking sheet or flat pan and freeze firm. Repack in freezing bags or cartons. When ready to use, spread out on baking sheet and bake in 400°F. oven 15 minutes. Serve hot.
Yield: About 3 dozen

Cheddar Chicken Puffs With Tarragon Sour Cream

1 can (11 ounces) **CAMPBELL'S Condensed Cheddar Cheese Soup**
1 can (5 ounces) **SWANSON Chunk Style Mixin' Chicken**
1 egg, slightly beaten
½ cup Italian flavored fine dry bread crumbs
2 tablespoons finely chopped green pepper
2 tablespoons finely chopped green onions
¼ teaspoon hot pepper sauce
Salad oil
¼ cup sour cream
Generous dash crushed tarragon leaves

In bowl, mix *thoroughly* ¼ cup soup, chicken, egg, bread crumbs, green pepper, green onions and hot pepper sauce. Shape into 40 small chicken meatballs (½ inch). Roll in additional bread crumbs. Half-fill deep fat fryer or large saucepan with oil; preheat to 350°F. Fry meatballs, a few at a time, in hot oil until browned. Drain; keep warm. Meanwhile, in saucepan, combine remaining soup, sour cream and tarragon. Heat; stir occasionally. Serve with meatballs. *Makes 40 appetizers*

Broccoli Puffs

10-oz. pkg. **GREEN GIANT® Cut Broccoli Frozen in Cheese Sauce**
1½ cups yellow cornmeal
½ cup flour
2 tablespoons sugar
1½ teaspoons garlic salt
1¼ teaspoons baking powder
1 teaspoon salt
¾ cup milk
1 egg
Oil for deep frying

(Continued)

(Continued)

Cook broccoli according to package directions. Empty contents into small bowl and cut broccoli, using 2 knives, into ½-inch pieces. Lightly spoon flour into measuring cup; level off. In medium bowl, combine cornmeal, flour, sugar, garlic salt, baking powder and salt. Stir in broccoli with cheese sauce, milk and egg; batter should be fairly thick. Allow batter to set 5 to 10 minutes. In deep fat fryer or heavy saucepan drop batter by teaspoonfuls into 1 to 1½-inches hot fat (375°F.). Fry until golden brown, turning once. Drain on paper towel.   *48 appetizers*

Star-Kist Tuna

Tuna Cheese Puff

1 cup milk
¼ cup butter or margarine
¼ teaspoon salt
Dash of pepper
1 cup sifted all-purpose flour
4 eggs
1 can (6½ or 7 ounces) STAR-KIST® Tuna, drained and flaked
½ cup (4 ounces) finely diced Swiss cheese, divided
1 tablespoon heavy cream
1 egg, beaten

In a medium saucepan, combine milk, butter, salt and pepper. Bring mixture to a boil. Remove from heat. Add flour all at once. Mix well. Stir in eggs, one at a time, blending well after each. Stir in STAR-KIST® Tuna, ¼ cup Swiss cheese and heavy cream. Spread batter into a greased 9-inch pie plate. Brush the top with beaten egg, sprinkle with remaining ¼ cup Swiss cheese. Bake in a 325° oven 40 to 50 minutes until puffed and brown.

Yield: 6 to 8 appetizer servings

General Mills

Chili-Cheese Rounds

1 can (16 ounces) refried beans
¼ cup finely chopped onion
1 teaspoon red pepper sauce
2 cups BISQUICK® Baking Mix
1 cup dairy sour cream
1 can (4 ounces) whole green chilies, drained, seeded and chopped
1 cup shredded Monterey Jack cheese (about 4 ounces)

Heat oven to 400°. Mix beans, onion and pepper sauce; reserve. Mix baking mix and sour cream until soft dough forms; beat vigorously 20 strokes. Gently smooth dough into ball on floured cloth-covered board. Knead 20 times. Roll dough ¼ inch thick. Cut with floured 2-inch cutter. Place on ungreased cookie sheet. Press a deep indentation about 1½ inches in diameter in center of each round with floured hands. Fill each with generous teaspoonful bean mixture; spread within indentation. Top each with chilies and cheese. Bake until light brown, 10 to 12 minutes.

About 30 appetizers

VARIATION:

Olive-Cheese Rounds

Substitute 1 can (2.2 ounces) sliced ripe olives (about ½ cup) for the chilies.

Sausage Rollups

1 (9-inch) BANQUET® Frozen Pie Crust Shell
½ pound bulk hot pork sausage

Pop frozen piecrust out of foil pan and place upside down on sheet of waxed paper to thaw, about 10 minutes. Flatten thawed pie crust by gently pressing down. Spread sausage evenly on top of crust to ½ inch from edge. Begin at one end and roll up pie crust jellyroll style. Cut off excess crust ½ inch from each end. Slice roll into ½-inch slices. Arrange slices with cut edge flat on cookie sheet. Bake in 350°F oven for 15 to 20 minutes, until crust is browned. Serve warm.   *Makes 12 pinwheel appetizers*

Pepperoni 'n Cheese Crescents

8-oz. can PILLSBURY Refrigerated Quick Crescent Dinner Rolls
24 slices pepperoni (1½-inch diameter) or 8 slices (3-inch diameter)
2 slices (4-inch diameter) KRAFT Natural Provolone or Low Moisture Part-Skim Mozzarella Cheese, quartered
1 egg white, slightly beaten

Heat oven to 375°F. Separate dough into 8 triangles. Place 3 slices of pepperoni, slightly overlapping, on center of each triangle; top each with quartered cheese slice. Roll up; start at shortest side of triangle and roll to opposite point. Place rolls point-side-down on ungreased cookie sheet; curve into crescent shape. Brush rolls with egg white. Bake at 375°F. for 10 to 14 minutes or until golden brown.   *8 snacks*

High Altitude—Above 3500 Feet: No change.

NUTRITION INFORMATION PER SERVING			
SERVING SIZE: ⅛ of recipe		Percent U.S. RDA	
Calories	170	Per Serving	
Protein	5 g	Protein	6%
Carbohydrate	13 g	Vitamin A	*
Fat	11 g	Thiamine	8%
Sodium	500 mg	Riboflavin	8%
Potassium	65 mg	Niacin	6%
		Calcium	6%
		Iron	4%

*Contains less than 2% of the U.S. RDA of this nutrient.

PILLSBURY BAKE-OFF® recipe

Famous Cheese Sizzlers

¼ cup DURKEE Imitation Bacon Bits
1½ cups shredded Swiss cheese
¼ cup DURKEE Famous Sauce
¼ cup DURKEE Stuffed Olives, chopped
1 tablespoon DURKEE Freeze-Dried Chives
24 slices party rye

Combine all ingredients except bread. Spread mixture on bread and cut into halves. Broil 4 inches from heat until cheese melts and is lightly brown.   *Makes 48 servings*

Cheezy Tater Crescent Snacks

2 (8-oz.) cans **PILLSBURY Refrigerated Quick Crescent Dinner Rolls**
½ cup **CHEEZ WHIZ Pasteurized Process Cheese Spread**
16 frozen potato nuggets, thawed
½ cup **PARKAY Margarine** or butter, melted
1 cup crushed herb seasoned croutons

Heat oven to 400°F. Grease 16 muffin cups. Separate dough into 16 triangles. Spread cheese evenly over each triangle. Place potato nugget on shortest side of each triangle. Roll up; start at shortest side of triangle and roll to opposite point. Pinch edges of dough to seal. Dip filled rolls in melted margarine; then in crushed croutons. Place in prepared muffin cups. Bake at 400°F. for 11 to 14 minutes or until golden brown. Serve hot.   *16 snacks*

Tip: To reheat, wrap loosely in foil; heat at 350°F. for 10 to 15 minutes.

High Altitude—Above 3500 Feet: No change.

NUTRITION INFORMATION PER SERVING
SERVING SIZE: 1/16 of recipe

		Percent U.S. RDA Per Serving	
Calories	210		
Protein	4 g	Protein	6%
Carbohydrate	19 g	Vitamin A	6%
Fat	13 g	Vitamin C	*
Sodium	655 mg	Thiamine	6%
Potassium	80 mg	Riboflavin	4%
		Niacin	4%
		Calcium	4%
		Iron	2%

*Contains less than 2% of the U.S. RDA of this nutrient.
PILLSBURY BAKE-OFF® recipe

Smoked Sausage Appetizers

Spread party rye bread with butter, then with mustard. Arrange three thin slices **ECKRICH® Smoked Sausage** on each slice. Sprinkle with small amount of grated mozzarella cheese. Broil until cheese is melted and sausage is heated through. Spear an olive with a party pick on each sandwich.
One pound of Smoked Sausage will make 16-18 sandwiches

Hidden Treasures

1 can (3 oz.) **BinB® Mushroom Crowns,** drained—reserving broth
1 package (10 oz.) refrigerator biscuits
¼ cup grated Parmesan cheese

Drain buttery broth from mushrooms. Reserve broth. Blot excess moisture from mushroom crowns with paper towels. Separate biscuits and cut each one into fourths. On floured board, press biscuit quarters into rounds and wrap one around each crown. Brush wrapped mushrooms with buttery broth and roll in Parmesan cheese. Bake on greased cookie sheet in preheated 400°F. oven for 10-12 minutes.   *Makes about 2 dozen appetizers*

Hot Chicken and Cheese Canapés

1 can (5 ounces) **SWANSON Chunk Chicken**
¼ cup shredded Cheddar cheese
¼ cup chopped celery
3 tablespoons mayonnaise
1 tablespoon chopped parsley
⅛ teaspoon hot pepper sauce

Combine ingredients; spread on crackers or toast squares. Broil 4" from heat until cheese melts.   *Makes about 1 cup*

General Mills

Cheesy Walnut Pinwheels

1 cup **BISQUICK® Baking Mix**
¼ cup cold water
1 package (3 ounces) cream cheese, softened
1 tablespoon mayonnaise or salad dressing
¼ cup shredded Cheddar cheese
¼ cup finely chopped walnuts
2 tablespoons finely chopped onions

Mix baking mix and water until soft dough forms; beat vigorously 20 strokes. Gently smooth dough into ball on floured cloth-covered board. Knead 5 times. Roll dough into rectangle, 12 × 9 inches.

Mix remaining ingredients; spread over dough to within ¼ inch of edges. Roll up tightly, beginning at 12-inch side. Seal well by pinching edge of dough into roll. Wrap and refrigerate until thoroughly chilled, at least 2 hours.

Heat oven to 400°. Cut roll into ¼-inch slices. Arrange slices, cut sides down, on greased cookie sheet. Bake until golden brown, 10 to 12 minutes.   *About 40 appetizers*

Bite-Sized Stuffies

1 loaf **RHODES™ Frozen Bread Dough,** thawed
36 cubes of ham, luncheon meats, cheese, shrimp, or stuffed olives
Melted butter
Parmesan cheese

Let dough rise slightly. Divide into thirds; then divide each third into 12 pieces. Shape each piece around meat, cheese, shrimp, or stuffed olive; seal well. Dip in melted butter, then Parmesan cheese. Place on greased cookie sheet. Cover; let rise in warm place until light or doubled in size, 30 to 60 minutes. Bake at 400°F. for 10 to 12 minutes. Serve warm.

Fireside Snack

Top **PREMIUM Saltine Crackers** with American cheese and miniature frankfurters. Toast in toaster-oven until cheese is melted.

Canapé Virginienne

Sliced tomato
American or Old English cheese
AMBER BRAND Deviled SMITHFIELD Ham
Slices of toast

Spread toast with **Deviled SMITHFIELD Ham** and cut in 1″ squares. Cover with 1″ squares of cheese. Set under broiler until cheese melts. Top with quarter slices of grilled tomato.

Broccoli Quiche

Crust:
1 cup **3 MINUTE BRAND® Quick Oats** or 3 packets Regular Flavor **HARVEST BRAND® Instant Oatmeal**
1 cup all-purpose flour
½ teaspoon salt
½ cup butter or margarine

Filling:
3 eggs
½ cup milk or light cream
⅔ cup chopped broccoli
⅔ cup shredded Swiss cheese
½ cup cooked and diced ham
1 tablespoon finely chopped onion or minced dried onion

CRUST:
Stir together oats, flour and salt. Cut in butter till crumbly. Pat dough in bottom and up sides of a quiche dish or 9-inch pie plate; set aside.

FILLING:
Combine eggs and milk; mix well. Stir in remaining ingredients. Pour into prepared crust. Bake in a 350°F. oven for 35 to 40 minutes or till a knife inserted near center comes out clean. Let stand 10 minutes before cutting into wedges.

Makes 6 main-dish servings

Note: To make **Bite-size Broccoli Quiches**, follow the above recipe *except* double all crust ingredients and pat dough in bottom and up sides of 1¾-inch muffin cups. Spoon about 1 tablespoon filling in each cup, and bake in a 350°F. oven about 20 minutes.

Makes 32 appetizers

ARGO®/KINGSFORD'S®
Mini Spinach Quiches

1 package (10 oz.) flaky refrigerator biscuits
3 tablespoons **ARGO®/KINGSFORD'S® Corn Starch**
¼ teaspoon ground nutmeg
¼ teaspoon salt
⅛ teaspoon pepper
1½ cups milk
1 egg, lightly beaten
1 cup shredded Swiss cheeese
1 package (10 oz.) frozen chopped spinach, cooked, well-drained

Separate each biscuit into 3 layers. Fit layers into 30 (1¾ x 1-inch) muffin pan cups. In 2-quart saucepan stir together corn starch,

nutmeg, salt and pepper. Gradually stir in milk until smooth. Stirring constantly, bring to boil over medium heat and boil 1 minute. Remove from heat. Gradually stir about ¼ cup of the hot corn starch mixture into the beaten egg until blended. Stir egg mixture into remaining hot mixture in pan. Cool. Stir in cheese and spinach. Spoon about 2 teaspoons spinach mixture into each tart. Bake in 400°F oven 15 minutes or until lightly browned. Remove from pan. Serve immediately. *Makes 30*

Note: Baked quiches may be frozen. Store in tightly covered container. Freeze up to 1 month. To reheat, place on cookie sheet and bake frozen quiches in 400°F oven 15 to 20 minutes or until heated through.

Quiche

12 slices **RATH® BLACK HAWK Bacon**, cut into small pieces and browned
1 cup shredded Swiss cheese
½ cup minced onions
4 eggs
2 cups light cream
Dash sugar
4-5 drops hot pepper sauce
Pastry for 1 crust, 9-10 inch pie, uncooked

Sprinkle **RATH® BLACK HAWK Bacon**, Swiss cheese and onion into pastry-lined pie pan. Beat eggs together, stir in light cream, sugar and hot pepper sauce. Pour over bacon, cheese and onions. Bake in 375° F. oven 50 to 55 minutes or until knife inserted into pie comes out clean. Let stand 5 to 10 minutes before cutting into wedges.

Mini-Quiches

1 can (8 oz.) refrigerated butterflake dinner rolls
1 pkg. (8 oz.) **OSCAR MAYER Ham and Cheese Spread**
2 eggs
2 green onions with tops, chopped

Separate dinner rolls into twelve pieces. Divide each piece into three sections. Press dough sections in 1¾-inch diameter tart or muffin cups, stretching dough slightly to form shell. Combine cheese spread, eggs and onion; mix well. Divide mixture evenly among shells. Bake in 375°F oven for 15 min. or until golden brown. Freeze extras; reheat on baking sheet in 350°F oven for 15 min.

Makes 36

Stagecoach Nachos

Spread **WOLF® Brand Chili** straight from the can onto tortilla chips, top with Cheddar cheese and heat in 300° oven until cheese melts. Spoon on picante sauce.

 **AZTECA**

Azteca® Nachos

Fresh Azteca® Nacho Chips

Cut **AZTECA® Corn Tortillas** into quarters and let dry in open air at least ½ hour. Fry in ¼″ hot oil or deep fat fry until golden brown.

Nachos Con Queso

Place fresh **AZTECA®** Nacho Chips on a cookie sheet. Top each with 1 Tbsp. shredded Cheddar and a small piece of canned jalapeño pepper. Heat 350° for 3 minutes.

Nachos Refrito

Place fresh **AZTECA®** Nacho Chips on a cookie sheet. Spread with refried beans. Top with 1 Tbsp. shredded Cheddar, piece of jalapeño and a dab of sour cream. Heat 350° for 3 minutes.

Nachos Ranchero

Place fresh **AZTECA®** Nacho Chips on a cookie sheet. Top each with 1 tsp. Salsa Ranchero* and 1 Tbsp. shredded Cheddar. Heat 350° for 3 minutes.

*Salsa Ranchero

Melt in Saucepan:

   3 Tbsp. melted butter or margarine

Fry:

   1 clove garlic, minced
   1 green pepper, seeded and chopped
   1 medium onion, chopped

Add:

   1 16 oz. can tomatoes
   1 jalapeño pepper (canned), rinsed in cold water and chopped
   ¼ tsp. salt
   Dash fresh ground pepper

Cook 15 minutes. This sauce can be used as a dip for fried tortilla chips. Store in refrigerator.

 **Nalley®**

Nalley®'s Nachos

NALLEY®'S Tortilla Chips
2 to 4 tablespoons diced **NALLEY®'S Jalapeno Peppers** or **NALLEY®'S Hot Chili Peppers**
1 4-ounce can sliced or chopped olives
½ pound shredded or sliced Muenster or Jack cheese
Guacamole, sour cream and picante sauce or salsa

Spread single layer of tortilla chips on baking sheet. Sprinkle evenly with peppers, olives and cheese. Broil about 4-inches from heat until cheese is melted, about 1½ to 2 minutes. Serve hot with guacamole, sour cream and picante sauce or salsa.

Jimmy Dean® Nachos

1 lb. **JIMMY DEAN® Seasoned Taco Filling**
2 Tbsp. tomato paste
1 bag tortilla chips
1 cup Cheddar cheese
Jalapeños to taste

Sauté **JIMMY DEAN® Seasoned Taco Filling** until brown and crumbly. Add 2 Tbsp. tomato paste. Spread on tortilla chips. Top with grated cheese. Broil till melted. Garnish with jalapeño. Optional: Top with 1 tsp. guacamole.

 JENO's

Snack Roll Nachos

Pile 1 cup refried beans in center of pizza pan, flatten beans. Top with 2 cups shredded Jack or Cheddar cheese, diced green chiles, sliced black olives and sliced green peppers. Place 24 **JENO'S® Mexican Style Snack Rolls** around pan. Bake at 375°F. for 15 minutes until dip is hot and cheese melted.

Cocktail Tostadas
(Tohs-Tah-Dahs)

   Small round fried corn tortillas (3 inch) or packaged tortilla chips
   1 can refried beans
   1 lb. **JIMMY DEAN® Taco Filling**
   Guacamole
   2 large tomatoes
   Shredded lettuce
   Parmesan or other grated cheese
   Jalapeños, sliced

Optional (additional garnishes):
   Sour cream
   Taco sauce or picante sauce

Brown taco filling as directed. Drain on paper towels. Spread on each tortilla about 1 Tbsp. refried beans. Top with 1 Tbsp. meat mixture. Add a few pieces of tomato, a layer of lettuce and a mound of guacamole. Garnish with cheese and a slice of jalapeño. Add sour cream and taco or picante sauce if desired.

Nacho Franks

   5 Tortillas*
   Oil for frying
   8 ounces Colby Cheese, grated
   Cocktail Sausages or Hot Dogs, sliced
   One 4-ounce can Jalapeño Chiles or Sauce

Cut tortillas into eighths and fry in oil until crisp, draining well on paper towels. Set aside. Arrange the fried tortilla chips on a cookie sheet. Cut and arrange a generous cube of cheese on each tortilla chip. Add a slice of hot dog or half a cocktail sausage and a small slice of hot pepper. Stick under the broiler for a few minutes until the cheese is melted and toasty. Serve immediately.

Yield: about 40 nachos

*Note: Tortilla Chips can also be ordered from any Mexican Restaurant, and are also available in packages at grocery stores.

Favorite recipe from the **National Hot Dog & Sausage Council**

Cheesy Tostada Appetizers

Cut one package **VAN DE KAMP'S® Corn Tortillas** in triangles and fry them in a small amount of oil until crisp. While still hot, salt to taste. After having cooled the tortilla chips, place grated Cheddar cheese or your favorite cheese on top of each chip. For an attractive accent, place a slice of black olive on top of the cheese and heat in the broiler until the cheese melts.

Tortilla Cheese Rolls

1 (5 oz.) jar process cheese spread with jalapeños
1½ cups (6 oz.) **SARGENTO Shredded Colby Cheese**
4 (8-inch) flour tortillas
1 (4 oz.) jar sliced pimientos, drained well
1 (4 oz.) can diced green chilies, drained

Combine cheeses in bowl or food processor fitted with plastic blade. Spread one tortilla evenly with ¼ of cheese mixture to within ½ inch of border. Top with second tortilla then spread with ¼ more of cheese mixture and sprinkle with ½ of green chilies and ½ of sliced pimientos. Roll tortillas as tightly as possible being careful not to let tortilla slide forward. Finished roll should be about 2 inches in diameter. Wrap tightly in foil.

Make second roll using remaining ingredients. Place wrapped rolls in refrigerator and chill at least 3 hours or overnight. Remove foil and slice rolls into ¼ inch thick rounds. Place on greased baking sheets and bake in 375° oven for 15 to 20 minutes, or until lightly crisp on top. *Makes about 24 appetizers*

THE ORIGINAL WORCESTERSHIRE

Empañadas
(Argentine Beef Turnovers)

1 package (8 oz.) cream cheese, softened
½ cup butter or margarine, softened
1½ cups all-purpose flour
1 tablespoon olive or salad oil
2 tablespoons minced onion
½ pound ground lean beef
1 can (8¼ oz.) tomatoes, drained and crushed
2 tablespoons chopped raisins
2 tablespoons chopped pitted green olives
1 tablespoon **LEA & PERRINS Worcestershire Sauce**
½ teaspoon salt
½ teaspoon oregano leaves, crumbled
1 hard-cooked egg, chopped
1 egg yolk
1 tablespoon water
¼ cup sesame seed

In the large bowl of an electric mixer blend cream cheese and butter. Gradually add flour; blend until dough is smooth. Divide dough into 3 balls; cover and chill until firm, about 30 minutes.

In a medium skillet heat oil. Add onion; sauté for 3 minutes. Add meat; cook and stir until browned, about 5 minutes. Stir in tomatoes, raisins, olives, **LEA & PERRINS**, salt, and oregano. Simmer, uncovered, for 5 minutes, stirring occasionally. Stir in chopped egg; cool.

On a lightly floured board roll each ball of dough separately to ⅛-inch thickness. With a 3-inch biscuit cutter, cut out circles. Spoon about 1 teaspoon of the meat mixture onto one side of each circle. Moisten edges with water; fold pastry over filling to form a semicircle; press edges to seal; crimp with fork tines. Repeat. Prick tops of turnovers to allow steam to escape. Mix egg yolk with water; brush over tops of turnovers. Sprinkle with sesame seed. Place on cookie sheets. Bake in a preheated hot oven (400 F.) until golden, about 12 minutes. Serve hot.

About 4 dozen

THE CHRISTIAN BROTHERS®
Empañada Grande

Pastry Dough*
1 cup chopped onions
1 large clove garlic, pressed
1 tablespoon vegetable oil
1 pound lean ground beef
½ cup diced tart apple
1 cup diced cooked potato
¾ cup **THE CHRISTIAN BROTHERS® Brandy**
¼ cup raisins
2 teaspoons grated orange peel
1 teaspoon salt
½ to 1 teaspoon dried red pepper flakes
⅛ teaspoon cinnamon
⅛ teaspoon ground cloves
1 egg, beaten

Prepare Pastry Dough; cover and chill. In large skillet over medium heat sauté onions and garlic in oil 5 minutes. Break up and add beef. Cook and stir until beef loses pink color. Drain fat. Add apple; cook and stir 5 minutes. Add potato, ½ cup of the brandy, the raisins, orange peel and seasonings. Cook and stir 5 to 8 minutes until liquid is absorbed. Stir in remaining ¼ cup brandy; cook 2 minutes. Set aside. Divide Pastry Dough in half. On lightly floured board roll one of the halves into a 10-inch circle. Transfer to baking sheet. Mound beef mixture onto center, leaving a 2-inch pastry border. Roll ¾ of the remaining pastry dough into a 9-inch circle. Place over meat mixture. Fold over and crimp edges to seal completely. Roll out the remaining dough and cut into desired shapes for decorating top of empañada. Apply decorations, using some of the egg for "glue," then brush top with egg and prick with fork. Bake in 375 degree oven 40 to 45 minutes until browned. Serve warm, cut into wedges.

Makes 8 to 10 appetizer servings

*Pastry Dough

In large bowl combine 2 cups flour, 1 teaspoon baking powder and ½ teaspoon salt. Cut in ⅔ cup vegetable shortening until mixture resembles coarse meal. Add 3 to 4 tablespoons water; toss with fork and form into a ball; wrap and chill.

Cheese Crescents
(Quesadillas)

Thoroughly moisten one side of an **AZTECA® Corn** or **Flour Tortilla** with water. On wet side, place 2 Tbsp. shredded Cheddar. Fold in half and fry until crisp in ½" hot oil. Press edges firmly together with tongs while frying. *(Continued)*

Spicy Crescents

Add **peppers**, **pepperoni** or **salami** with cheese.

Appetizer Crescents

Cut tortillas in half then make as above.

Cheese Sandwiches

Make as above, but do not fry. Fasten edges with a toothpick and place on cookie sheet. Cover with foil. Heat in 300° oven for 10 minutes.

Fried Mozzarella

16 ounces **MIGLIORE®** Mozzarella
½ cup all-purpose flour
2 eggs, lightly beaten
Salt & pepper to taste
1 cup bread crumbs
1 cup olive oil

Cut **MIGLIORE®** Mozzarella into small squares, roll in flour, dip in egg seasoned with salt and pepper, roll in bread crumbs, dip in egg again and roll in bread crumbs. Fry in hot olive oil just long enough for bread crumbs to turn golden brown. Serve hot.

6 servings

Crisco
Fried Cheese Cubes

Assorted natural cheeses, cut in ½-inch cubes*
Beaten egg
Fine dry bread crumbs
CRISCO® for deep frying

If using soft cheeses, shape crust around the soft center as much as possible. Dip cheese cubes in beaten egg, then coat with crumbs. Repeat dipping in egg and crumbs for a second layer. (A thick coating prevent cheese from leaking through during frying.) Fry, a few cubes at a time in deep **CRISCO®** heated to 365° till cubes are golden, about ½ minute. Serve warm.

*Use soft cheeses with a crust (Camembert or Brie), semi-hard cheeses (Bel Paese or brick), or hard cheeses (Cheddar, Edam, and Gouda).

Wheat Germ Herb Balls

1¾ cups unsifted **ROBIN HOOD®** All Purpose Flour
½ cup **KRETSCHMER** Regular Wheat Germ
2 cups grated sharp Cheddar cheese
1 cup softened butter or margarine
¾ tsp. thyme leaves, crushed
¼ tsp. dry mustard
Wheat germ for topping

Combine flour and ½ cup wheat germ on wax paper. Stir to blend. Beat cheese, butter, thyme and mustard together until well-blended. Add blended dry ingredients to cheese mixture, mixing to combine. Shape into 1-inch balls. Dip half of each ball in remaining wheat germ. Place dipped-side up on ungreased baking sheets.

Bake at 400° for 10-12 minutes until lightly browned. Remove from baking sheet. Cool on rack.   *Makes 4½ dozen appetizers*

Spinach Balls

2 packages (10 ounces each) Frozen **STOKELY'S®** **Chopped Spinach**
2 medium-size onions, chopped
6 eggs, unbeaten
2 cups herb-seasoned stuffing mix
½ cup grated Parmesan cheese
¼ cup butter or margarine, melted
1 teaspoon salt
1 Tablespoon garlic salt
½ teaspoon thyme
Pepper to taste

Preheat oven to 350°F. Thaw spinach and place in large sieve. Drain spinach thoroughly, squeezing out as much water as possible. Add spinach to remaining ingredients; mix well. Shape mixture into balls the size of walnuts. Bake on greased jelly-roll pan 20 minutes. Serve promptly.   *About 60 appetizers*

Note: Spinach balls may be wrapped and frozen, then thawed 1 hour before baking.

Bacon Tater Tots® Bites

1. According to the number of snacks needed, cook half strips of bacon until lightly browned but still limp.
2. Meanwhile, prepare frozen **ORE-IDA® TATER TOTS®*** according to package directions.
3. Cut slices of American Cheese into thirds; wrap a strip of cheese around hot **TATER TOTS®**. Wrap limp bacon around cheese and secure both with toothpicks.
4. Broil, turning "bites" once, until bacon is crisp.
5. Serve hot with Mustard Sauce (recipe follows).

Note: Bites can be assembled and refrigerated. Just before serving, broil, to crisp bacon and rewarm the **TATER TOTS®**.

*May be used with the following **ORE-IDA®** products:

TATER TOTS® With Bacon Flavored Vegetable **Protein**
TATER TOTS® With Onions

Mustard Sauce

Blend together ½ cup **HEINZ Mustard**, ¼ cup brown sugar and ½ teaspoon ginger.

Baked Appetizer Tray

Put 1-16 oz. can of beanless chili into 8-inch cake pan. Top with 2 cups shredded Jack or Cheddar cheese. Surround with 12 to 36 **JENO'S®** Mexican Style Snack Rolls on a baking sheet. Bake at 375°F. for 15 minutes until Rolls sizzle and cheese is melted.

Serves 6 to 10

Scotch Eggs

¾ pound bulk pork sausage
12 hard-cooked eggs
1 egg, beaten
⅓ cup fine dry bread crumbs
Fat for deep frying

Divide sausage into 12 equal portions (1 oz. each). Shape each portion into patty and wrap completely around 1 hard-cooked egg, pressing edges together to seal. Dip sausage-wrapped eggs in beaten egg; then roll in bread crumbs until completely coated. Cook eggs in preheated 375°F. deep fat until golden brown and heated through, 7 to 9 minutes. Drain on absorbent paper. Serve hot or cold.   *6 servings*

Favorite recipe from the **American Egg Board**

Hot First Course Appetizers

Bertolli® Stuffed Artichokes

4 medium artichokes
Juice of 1 lemon
1 rib celery, thinly sliced
½ red pepper, cut into strips
¼ cup finely chopped onion
1 tablespoon **BERTOLLI® Olive Oil**
1 cup cooked peas
2 tablespoons walnut pieces
¼ cup **BERTOLLI® Olive Oil**
1 tablespoon **BERTOLLI® Red Wine Vinegar**
1 teaspoon sugar
Dash each salt and pepper

Cut stem and 1-inch top from artichokes; cut tips off leaves. Rub artichokes with lemon juice; heat to boiling in 2-inches water in saucepan. Reduce heat; simmer covered until tender, about 30 minutes. Drain; cool. Separate top leaves; remove chokes with spoon.

Sauté celery, pepper and onion in 1 tablespoon oil in skillet 4 minutes. Stir in peas and walnuts. Mix remaining ingredients; stir into vegetables. Spoon vegetables into center of artichokes. Serve hot or refrigerate and serve cold.   *Makes 4 servings*

Broiled Ruby Reds

2 **TEXAS RUBY RED Grapefruit**, halved
¼ cup **IMPERIAL Brown Sugar**
¼ teaspoon cinnamon
¼ cup shredded coconut
Maraschino cherries

Cut around each section with grapefruit knife. Combine **IMPERIAL Brown Sugar** and cinnamon and spread over grapefruit. Broil until juice is bubbling. Sprinkle with shredded coconut and broil until coconut is toasted. Add cherries to centers of grapefruit.   *Makes 4 servings*

Favorite recipe from the **Texas Citrus Industry**

Grapefruit Deluxe
(Low Calorie)

1 grapefruit
Artificial sweetener to equal 2 teaspoons sugar
¼ teaspoon cinnamon
¼ teaspoon **ANGOSTURA® Aromatic Bitters**

Cut grapefruit in half. Loosen each section from skin and membrane. Sprinkle sweetener, cinnamon and **ANGOSTURA® Bitters** over each half. Bake at 350° F. (moderate oven) for 4 minutes or until heated throughout.   *Yield: 2 Servings*

Broiled Grapefruit Toppings

Top each **SUNKIST® Grapefruit** half with **one** of the following:

2 tsp. brown sugar
1 Tbsp. maple-flavored syrup *or* apricot preserves
2 tsp. orange, almond *or* coffee-flavored liqueur
2 tsp. sugar and 1 tsp. rum
2 tsp. sugar and dash ground cinnamon
1 Tbsp. *each* peanut butter and honey
1 Tbsp. *each* brown sugar and chopped nuts

Place in broiler 4 to 5 inches from source of heat. Broil until bubbly (cold broiler 6 to 8 minutes **or** preheated broiler 3 to 4 minutes).

Milwaukee Salami Cups

12 slices salami
1 can (16 oz.) **VEG-ALL® Mixed Vegetables**, drained
½ cup shredded cheese
1 teaspoon prepared mustard
3 eggs, slightly beaten
¾ cup milk
¼ teaspoon salt

Fit salami slices into 12 wells of lightly-greased muffin pan. Spoon equal amount of **VEG-ALL®** in each cup. Stir cheese with mustard; top **VEG-ALL®** in each cup with about a half teaspoon of the cheese mixture. Combine eggs, milk and salt. Pour the egg mixture into each filled salami cup. Bake in a preheated 350°F. oven 25 to 30 minutes.   *Serves 6*

The Brothers Prawns

1 large clove garlic, chopped
¼ medium onion, chopped
2 tablespoons olive oil
½ lb. prawns, shelled and deveined
Salt and pepper to taste
2 teaspoons flour
⅔ cup **THE CHRISTIAN BROTHERS® Chablis**
2 tablespoons **THE CHRISTIAN BROTHERS® Brandy**
2 tablespoons minced parsley

Sauté garlic and onion in olive oil over medium-high heat until limp. Add prawns and sauté over high heat for 1 minute or until pink. Season with salt and pepper. Add flour and toss to mix. Add chablis and brandy and boil, uncovered, 4 minutes or until sauce is reduced and glossy. Mix in parsley.   *Makes 4 servings*

King Crab Royal

10 to 12 ounces **ALASKA King Crab** split legs, thawed if necessary
¼ cup butter, melted
1 tablespoon lemon juice
2 teaspoons grated onion
1 clove garlic, crushed
1 tablespoon finely chopped parsley
¼ teaspoon *each* salt and crushed tarragon
Dash bottled hot pepper sauce

Remove crab meat from shells and cut into bite-size pieces for easier serving; return to shells. Combine remaining ingredients and brush over crab. Broil 3 to 5 inches from heat 3 to 4 minutes; brush occasionally with sauce.

Makes 4 main dish servings or 8 appetizer servings
Favorite recipe from the **Alaska Seafood Marketing Institute**

Shrimp Filled Pancakes

8-10 thin pancakes
3-4 tablespoons butter
1¼ tablespoons flour
1¼ cups fish or vegetable stock
2 egg yolks
⅓ cup cream
¼ teaspoon salt
Dash of white pepper
1 tablespoon lemon juice
½ lb. shrimp
3 tablespoons chopped dill
4-6 tablespoons grated **FINLANDIA Swiss**

Blend 2 tablespoons melted butter and the flour in saucepan. Gradually add fish or vegetable stock stirring constantly and let simmer for a few minutes. Beat together cream and eggs. Stir a little of the hot sauce into this mixture. Add to the sauce, stirring vigorously. Let the sauce simmer, stirring constantly until it thickens. Remove from fire and add butter (1-2 tablespoons) in small pieces. Finally add seasoning, shrimp and dill.

Divide the mixture on each pancake. Roll the pancakes and arrange in a greased baking dish. Sprinkle with grated cheese and dot with butter. Bake in oven (375°) for about 10 minutes and serve as hors d'oeuvres.   *Makes 4 servings*

Cold First Course Appetizers

Shrimp Cocktail

2 lbs. **ATALANTA Shrimp**, raw, shelled, deveined

Bring salted water (1 tsp. salt per quart of water) to a boil in a kettle. Add the shrimp. When water reboils cook shrimp 3-4 minutes. Chill and serve with cocktail sauce or Dill Sauce.*

Yield: 8 Servings

*Dill Sauce

1 cup Sour cream
1 tsp. Dried dill or 1 Tbsp. Fresh dillweed
3 Tbsp. Lemon juice

Mix well sour cream, dill and lemon juice.

Doused Shrimp*

2 pounds medium-size raw shrimp
1 quart water
1 lemon, thinly sliced
1 red onion, thinly sliced
½ cup pitted black olives
2 tablespoons chopped pimiento
½ cup lemon juice
¼ cup oil
2 tablespoons **LEA & PERRINS Worcestershire Sauce**
1 clove garlic, crushed
1 teaspoon salt
⅛ teaspoon **TABASCO®**

Peel and devein shrimp. In a saucepan bring water to a boil. Add shrimp and cook for 3 minutes. Drain at once and place in serving bowl. Add the lemon, onion, olives and pimiento; toss gently. In a small bowl combine lemon juice, oil, **LEA & PERRINS**, garlic, salt and **TABASCO®**; mix well. Stir this marinade into the shrimp mixture. Cover; refrigerate at least 2 hours, stirring occasionally. Serve on lettuce-lined plates, if desired.   *Yield: 1 quart*

*May be prepared in advance of serving.

Shrimp Cocktails for Four

1 can (4½ ounces) **LOUISIANA BRAND Shrimp**
1 tablespoon lemon juice
Lettuce

Sauce:
⅔ cup chili sauce or tomato catsup
1 tablespoon prepared horseradish
1 tablespoon lemon juice
⅓ cup chopped celery

Drain shrimp. Cover with ½ cup cold water; add lemon juice. Refrigerate 2 hours or longer. Drain well; arrange in cocktail glasses on crisp lettuce. Combine sauce ingredients; serve over shrimp.

Rock Lobster Petites With Caper Mayonnaise

Drop 12 frozen **SOUTH AFRICAN ROCK LOBSTER Petites (2 oz. size)** into boiling salted water. When water reboils, cook tails 2 minutes. Drain immediately and drench with cold water. Cut away underside membrane and remove meat in one piece. Reserve shells. Cut rock lobster into crosswise slices. Arrange slices in shell. Mix ½ cup mayonnaise with ⅔ cup sour cream, and 3 tablespoons each of catsup and drained capers. Serve with petites.

Favorite recipe from **South African Rock Lobster Service Corp.**

Seviche con Two Fingers®

½ cup lemon juice
½ cup lime juice
½ cup **TWO FINGERS® Tequila**
2 small dried red chili peppers
1 clove garlic, pressed or diced
1 teaspoon salt
Dash dill weed
1 pound sole, halibut or any white flesh fish
1 sweet red onion, sliced
Lettuce

Combine lemon and lime juice with tequila. Seed peppers, and finely grind. Add to first mixture, along with garlic, salt and dill. Cut fish in 1-inch pieces, and pour the mixture over. Top with onion slices. Cover and refrigerate for at least 3 hours, until fish is opaque. Serve as an appetizer or as a salad on lettuce.

Makes about 2⅔ cups

Note: The citrus juices have much the same effect on the white fish meat that boiling the meat does, so it is essentially "cooked."

DANNON® YOGURT
Cucumber Appetizer

1 large cucumber, peeled, pitted, sliced
Salt
1 cup **DANNON® Plain Yogurt**
1 small onion, sliced
1 clove garlic, mashed
½ teaspoon fresh mint, chopped
Juice of ½ lemon
Lettuce leaves
Walnuts, for garnish

Season sliced cucumber with salt. Allow to stand for 10 to 15 minutes. Drain off any liquid residue. To cucumbers, add yogurt, sliced onion, garlic, mint and lemon juice. Toss well. Arrange on lettuce leaves and garnish with walnuts. *Serves 2 as appetizer*

Picture Perfect
Hors d'Oeuvre Wheel

1 (10-ounce) package piecrust mix
3 to 4 tablespoons cold water
¾ cup unflavored yogurt
1 teaspoon horseradish
¼ teaspoon garlic salt
⅛ teaspoon liquid hot pepper seasoning
1 (4⅝ ounce) can **SNACK MATE Pasteurized Process Cheese Spread,** any flavor
12 cherry tomatoes, tops removed and halved
1 small cucumber or zucchini, thinly sliced
¼ cup thinly sliced scallions

1. Prepare piecrust mix according to package directions, using cold water. Between 2 sheets of wax paper, roll dough into one 12-inch circle. Place dough on large cookie sheet, removing wax paper. Turn edge under slightly and crimp edge deeply. Prick with fork; chill 1 hour.
2. Preheat oven to 475°F.; bake crust 8 to 10 minutes. Cool completely on cookie sheet; place on serving platter
3. In small bowl, combine yogurt, horseradish, garlic salt and liquid hot pepper seasoning. Immediately before serving, spread evenly over bottom of pastry circle.
4. Make circle of **SNACK MATE Cheese** rosettes around edge of pastry circle, pressing cheese from nozzle of pressurized can. Arrange cherry tomato halves, cut side down, in circle inside cheese rosettes.
5. Arrange a circle of overlapping cucumber or zucchini slices inside cherry tomato halves; make a second circle of **SNACK MATE Cheese** rosettes next to cucumber. Arrange a circle of scallion slices and fill center with **SNACK MATE Cheese** rosettes. Cut into thin wedges to serve as a fork appetizer.

Makes 8 to 10 servings

Chinese Spiced Mushrooms

½ lb. fresh mushrooms, wiped clean, stem ends removed
1 quart boiling water
2 tablespoons **LA CHOY® Soy Sauce**
1 tablespoon sherry
Pinch salt
TABASCO® Sauce and sesame oil to taste
Crisp lettuce leaves

Place mushrooms in colander in sink; pour boiling water over to blanch. Drain and dry thoroughly. Combine soy sauce, sherry, salt, **TABASCO® Sauce** and sesame oil, mixing well. Add mushrooms and toss. Refrigerate to chill, about 20 minutes. Serve on crisp lettuce leaves. *4 Servings*

Jellied Appetizer
(Low Calorie)

1 tablespoon unflavored gelatin
1 cup tomato juice
1 cup dietetic lemon-flavored soda
1 tablespoon **ANGOSTURA® Aromatic Bitters**
½ teaspoon salt
1 cup shredded cabbage
4 large lettuce leaves

Sprinkle gelatin over tomato juice to soften. Cook over low heat, stirring constantly, until gelatin is dissolved. Remove from heat. Add lemon soda, **ANGOSTURA® Bitters** and salt. Chill until mixture is the consistency of unbeaten egg whites. Fold in shredded cabbage. Chill until set. Serve on lettuce leaves.

Yield: 4 servings

Cold Appetizers

Classic Caviar Serving

2 hard-boiled eggs, chopped fine
1 medium-size onion, minced
6-8 oz. sour cream (or yogurt)
Sweet butter (or margarine)
Thin-sliced brown bread, white toast triangles
Unsalted crackers
Seeded lemon wedges
3½-4 oz. **ROMANOFF® Caviar***

Chill caviar and present in original container or glass cup nestled in a bowl of cracked ice. Surround with individual dishes of the egg, sour cream, butter, onion and lemon wedges. Serve with the breads and crackers. Let guests mix-and-match caviar accompaniments. An ideal hors d'oeuvre with cocktails, iced vodka or well-chilled dry, white wine.

*Your choice of **ROMANOFF® Black** or **Red Lumpfish**, **Whitefish** or **Salmon Caviar**.

Steak Tartare

1 pound raw, ground beef (top round, sirloin or fillet)*
2 egg yolks
½ teaspoon salt
½ teaspoon Worcestershire sauce
¼ teaspoon pepper
½ cup finely chopped green onions or scallions
¼ cup finely chopped parsley
1 to 3 finely chopped anchovy fillets
Capers
Anchovy fillets
PEPPERIDGE FARM® Butter and Goldfish Thins Crackers

Mix beef, egg yolks, salt, Worcestershire sauce, pepper, onions and parsley. Add chopped anchovies to taste. Shape meat mixture into a ball; place on serving platter and flatten slightly. Garnish top with capers and anchovy fillets and surround with crackers.

Makes 8 to 10 servings

*Note: Have butcher grind meat at least three times.

Chicken Liver Pâté

2 fresh chicken livers
1 medium hard boiled egg
1 Tbsp. **FILIPPO BERIO Olive Oil**
1 medium sized onion
Salt and pepper

Slice onion and fry in **FILIPPO BERIO Olive Oil** until light brown. Put chicken livers in pan and fry together for about 4 more minutes. Put everything into a bowl and chop onion and liver together, adding salt and pepper to taste. When you form a good paste (pâté), slowly add a teaspoon of **FILIPPO BERIO Olive Oil** and continue mixing until right consistency. Serve on crackers or small squares of toasted bread.

Halftime Pâté

⅓ cup toasted chopped almonds
4 strips **WILSON® Bacon**, fried crisp and crumbled
½ cup mayonnaise
1½ cups grated sharp Cheddar cheese
1½ tablespoons finely chopped onion

Combine all ingredients in a small bowl. Serve with your favorite crackers.

Holland House®
Chicken Liver Pâté

Melt 3 Tbsp. butter or margarine in skillet. Sauté 1 lb. chicken livers with 1 cup finely chopped onions and 2 crushed garlic cloves. When livers lose pinkness, add ⅓ cup **HOLLAND HOUSE® Marsala Cooking Wine**. Cook approx. 2 mins. Remove from heat. Combine liver mixture with 3 oz. cream cheese, 1 Tbsp. butter, ½ tsp. tarragon, ½ tsp. dry mustard and dash Worcestershire sauce in electric blender. Mix until smooth. Pour into crock and chill before serving.

Party Country Pâté

1 pound finely ground pork
½ pound finely ground veal
⅔ cup finely chopped boiled ham
½ cup chopped black olives
½ cup ground blanched almonds
1 cup fresh bread crumbs
⅓ cup **B&B Liqueur**
1 egg
1 clove garlic, crushed
1 teaspoon rosemary
½ teaspoon salt
½ teaspoon thyme
1 tablespoon margarine or butter
Parsley

In a large bowl combine pork, veal, ham, olives and blanched almonds. Soften bread crumbs in **B&B Liqueur** and add with egg, garlic, rosemary, salt and thyme to meat mixture; thoroughly mix together.

Coat the bottom and sides of a 5-cup mold or an 8½ × 4½ × 2½-inch loaf pan with margarine. Fill with meat mixture, pressing down firmly. Bake at 350°F. for 1½ hours. Drain. Cover pâté with foil and weight down with a heavy can. Refrigerate 12 hours.

Unmold pâté onto serving plate. Serve pâté at room temperature, garnished with parsley sprigs. *Makes 1 4-cup mold*

Animex
Ham Pâté

2 cups minced **ATALANTA/KRAKUS/POLKA Polish Ham**
1 cup grated Swiss cheese
¼ cup finely chopped radishes
2 tablespoons finely chopped green onion
2 tablespoons sweet pickle relish
½ cup mayonnaise or salad dressing
1 teaspoon dry mustard
Toasted saltines
Chopped parsley

In a bowl, blend ham, cheese, radishes, onion, pickle relish, mayonnaise and mustard. Shape into a ball. Chill until ready to serve.

To toast saltines, place on cookie sheet and bake at 300°F. for 7 minutes, until golden brown.

To serve, roll in parsley; place on platter. Surround with crackers. *Makes 8 servings*

Quick Pâté

½ pound liverwurst
¼ cup **BEST FOODS®/HELLMANN'S® Real Mayonnaise**
½ teaspoon grated onion
Dash salt
Dash pepper

Mash liverwurst with fork. Blend **Real Mayonnaise**, onion, salt and pepper. *Makes about 1 cup*

To Frost: Press pâté into small bowl or 1 (10-ounce) custard cup. Chill several hours, until firm. Blend 2 ounces (¼ cup) cream cheese and 2 tablespoons **Real Mayonnaise**. Unmold pâté. Spread top and sides with cream cheese mixture. Chill. Garnish as desired.

For Larger Mold: Follow directions for Quick Pâté, increasing liverwurst to ¾ pound, **Real Mayonnaise** to ⅓ cup and grated onion to 1 teaspoon. Makes about 1½ cups. To frost, press pâté into (6 x 3½ x 2-inch) aluminum foil pan lined with waxed paper. Chill several hours, until firm. Blend 1 (3-ounce) package cream cheese and 2 tablespoons **Real Mayonnaise**. Unmold pâté. Spread top and sides with cream cheese mixture. Chill. Score top and garnish between the scores with slices stuffed olives.

Smoked Salmon Pâté

(Low Calorie)

	Calories
1—15½ oz. can **HUMPTY DUMPTY Chum Salmon***	554
⅔ cup low fat cottage cheese	140
¼ teaspoon liquid smoke flavoring	—
1 tablespoon lemon juice	4
2 tablespoons minced onion	8
2 tablespoons finely chopped ripe olives	36
1 teaspoon seasoned salt	—
1 teaspoon Worcestershire sauce	4
½ teaspoon paprika	—
	746

Drain salmon and chop very fine or mash with a fork. Press cottage cheese through sieve and combine with salmon and remaining ingredients. Mix well. Cover and chill for at least 1 hour. Serve with Melba toast or rye crackers. *Makes 2½ cups*

Calories per tablespoon = Approx. 18

*****GILLNETTERSBEST, DOUBLE Q** or **DEMING'S Salmon** may be subsituted.

TABASCO®
Shrimp Remoulade

½ cup Creole or brown mustard
½ cup salad oil
¼ cup catchup
¼ cup vinegar
¼ teaspoon **TABASCO® Pepper Sauce**
2 tablespoons *each* finely chopped celery, onion, and green pepper
1 pound cooked cleaned shrimp

Combine mustard, oil, catchup, vinegar, **TABASCO®**, celery, onion and green pepper. Mix until blended. Add shrimp, cover and chill. *Yield: About 3½ cups*

Rock Lobster in Aspic for a Buffet

12 (2 oz.) **SOUTH AFRICAN ROCK LOBSTER Tails**
4 cups chicken stock
Juice of 1 lemon
2 envelopes unflavored gelatine
⅓ cup chopped dill pickles
⅓ cup sliced celery
⅓ cup sliced stuffed olives
1 tablespoon chopped scallions
Salad greens

Drop frozen rock lobster tails into boiling salted water. When water reboils, cook for 2 minutes. Drain immediately, drench with cold water and cut away underside membrane. Remove meat in one piece. Combine chicken stock with lemon juice and measure out 1 cup into small saucepan. Add unflavored gelatine and let soak for 5 minutes. Dissolve over low heat and then add to remaining chicken stock. Chill until the consistency of egg whites. Fold in remaining ingredients except salad greens. Cut rock lobster tails in half lengthwise. Arrange tail halves decoratively in a lightly-oiled 6-8 cup mold. Add a little gelatine mixture to hold rock lobster in place. Chill until firm. Add remaining gelatine mixture and chill until firm. Unmold on platter. Surround with salad greens and serve with mayonnaise if desired.

Favorite recipe from the **South African Rock Lobster Service Corp.**

Holiday Ham Mold

½ cup water
1 tablespoon unflavored gelatin (1 envelope)
1 cup chicken broth, hot
1 stalk celery
1 quarter of medium onion
1 medium sweet pickle
¼ teaspoon cream-style horseradish
2 cans (4½ oz. each) deviled ham
⅔ cup prepared **HIDDEN VALLEY ORIGINAL RANCH® Salad Dressing**

In a medium bowl, mix gelatin with cold water. Add hot chicken broth and stir until gelatin is dissolved. Cool. In a blender or food processor chop celery, onion and pickle. Blend with horseradish and deviled ham. Stir in Salad Dressing and cooled gelatin mixture. Pour into a 2-cup mold. Refrigerate several hours. Serve, sliced thin, as an appetizer. *Makes 8 to 10 servings*

Dorman's® Muenster Mousse

½ envelope (1½ teaspoons) unflavored gelatine
¼ cup white wine
¼ cup boiling water
3 scallions, chopped
½ cup PLUS 1 tablespoon heavy cream
1 egg
1 teaspoon salt
1 tablespoon cognac, optional
3 slices **DORMAN'S® Muenster Cheese**
Sliced almonds

Sprinkle gelatine over wine; let stand until softened. Add boiling water; stir until dissolved. In electric blender container, combine dissolved gelatine and remaining ingredients except sliced almonds. Blend 10 seconds. Pour into a 1½ cup mold. Chill in refrigerator until firm. Unmold and garnish with sliced almonds.

Serves 6

Curried Almond Chicken Balls

½ cup **BLUE DIAMOND® Chopped Natural Almonds,** toasted
1 can (6½ ounces) boned chicken
1 package (3 ounces) cream cheese, softened
2 tablespoons chutney, chopped
1 teaspoon curry powder
Salt and pepper
Minced parsley

Finely chop almonds; set aside. In small bowl, mix together chicken and cream cheese, breaking up any large chunks of chicken. Add chutney, curry powder and almonds; mix until well-blended; salt and pepper to taste. Chill until mixture is firm, about one hour. Shape into 1-inch balls and roll in minced parsley. Chill until ready to serve.

Makes about 24 (1-inch) balls

Chicken Veronique Appetizers

¾ pound cooked chicken breast, in ¾-inch cubes
2 tablespoons sweet French dressing
¾ pound **THOMPSON Seedless Green Grapes**
1 package (3 oz.) cream cheese, softened
2 tablespoons orange juice concentrate
3 tablespoons sour cream
⅛ teaspoon bottled hot pepper sauce

Toss warm chicken in French dressing; refrigerate 2 hours. Drain well. On frilled toothpicks skewer 1 grape, 1 piece chicken and 1 more grape. Arrange on platter.

Beat cream cheese until fluffy; beat in orange juice concentrate, sour cream and hot pepper sauce. Serve with skewered chicken and grapes.

Makes 45 to 50 appetizers

Favorite recipe from the **California Table Grape Commission**

Cheese Stuffed Celery

Pipe 1 (4¾-ounce) can **SNACK MATE Pasteurized Process Cheese Spread Cheddar** onto 4 stalks celery. Cut into 1½-inch pieces. Stand a **CORN DIGGERS Snack** in end of each. Sprinkle with paprika, if desired.

Makes 24 (about 1½-inch) pieces

SKIPPY. Stuffed Celery

2 packages (3 oz. each) cream cheese
½ cup **SKIPPY® Creamy** or **Super Chunk Peanut Butter**
¼ cup sesame seeds, toasted
2 teaspoons milk
2 teaspoons soy sauce
¼ teaspoon ground ginger
Celery stalks

In small bowl stir cream cheese and peanut butter until blended; mix in sesame seeds, milk, soy sauce and ginger. Stuff celery stalks and cut to desired size. *Makes about 1½ cups*

Note: May also be served as a spread on crackers.

Buddig Stuffed Celery

1 3-ounce package cream cheese, softened
2 tablespoons blue cheese, crumbled
1 tablespoon cream
¼ cup chopped **BUDDIG Smoked Sliced Beef** or **Ham**
Celery sticks

Combine all ingredients, except celery. Dry celery and fill with beef mixture.

Stuffed Celery Elite

1 5-ounce jar bacon-cheese spread
1 package **FRITO-LAY® Brand Green Onion Dip Mix**
4 celery sticks

Combine cheese spread with **FRITO-LAY® Brand Green Onion Dip Mix**. (If mixture is too firm to spread, thin with 1 to 2 tablespoons milk.) Fill celery sticks with cheese spread. Chill and cut into desired lengths.

Kellogg's®
Freckle Logs

6 ribs celery
1 cup peanut butter
6 tablespoons **KELLOGG'S® BRAN BUDS® Cereal**
3 tablespoons raisins

Wash and trim celery. Cut into 4-inch pieces. Mix peanut butter and **KELLOGG'S® BRAN BUDS® Cereal**. Fill celery pieces with peanut butter mixture. Top with raisins.

Yield: about 18 pieces, 2 per serving

® Kellogg Company

Smokey Tidbits

Tuck slivers of smoked salmon inside big shiny black **LINDSAY® Pitted Ripe Olives**, add a tassel of parsley and serve on picks.

Cheesey Celery Snack

Combine: ½ lb. grated **CHEEZ-OLA®**, ¼ cup finely chopped ripe olives, 2 tablespoons chopped green pepper, dash of garlic powder, ½ cup safflower mayonnaise. Stuff celery stalks or serve on crackers or bread.

Tomato Teasers

1 pint cherry tomatoes
½ pound bacon, cooked and crumbled
¼ teaspoon **TABASCO®**

Cut out small hole in the top of each tomato. Combine crumbled bacon with **TABASCO®**. Spoon bacon mixture into tomatoes. Serve with food picks. *Yield: About 24 tomatoes*

Wild Rice Salad Appetizers

1 pkg. (6 oz.) **UNCLE BEN'S® Long Grain & Wild Rice**
1 cup finely diced cooked chicken or ham
½ cup finely chopped celery
2 tablespoons chopped green onion
1 tablespoon chopped parsley
⅓ cup salad dressing or mayonnaise
1 tablespoon lemon juice
Cherry tomatoes
Cucumber slices
Thin pimiento strips

Cook rice as directed on package. Chill. Add chicken or ham, celery, green onion, parsley, salad dressing and lemon juice; mix well. Chill. To fill tomatoes, cut a thin slice from top of washed tomatoes; remove seeds and drain well. Stuff tomatoes with salad mixture. Slice cucumber about ⅜ inch thick and top each slice with a heaping teaspoonful of salad mixture. Garnish with pimiento. *Makes 4 cups salad mixture.*
(About 1 cup salad mixture will fill 24 cherry tomatoes or top 24 cucumber slices.)

Tiny Tomato Pleasers

½ cup **SHOAL LAKE Pure Canadian Wild Rice**
1 pint cherry tomatoes
3-4 strips bacon
¼ teaspoon **TABASCO®** (optional)
½ cup mayonnaise

Cook wild rice according to basic package directions. Fry bacon crisp. Drain and crumble. Cut out small hole in top of each tomato and scoop out center. Combine bacon, wild rice, mayonnaise, and **TABASCO®**. Spoon mixture into tomatoes, serve on lettuce bed.
Fills 20-24 tomatoes

Millionaire Mushrooms

1 can (3 oz.) **BinB® Mushroom Crowns**, drained
1 jar (6 oz.) marinated artichoke hearts, undrained
1 tablespoon chopped pimiento

Combine crowns, artichoke hearts with liquid and pimiento. Cover and chill overnight; stir now and then. Drain and serve with wooden picks.

100% PURE
MinuteMaid®
Lemon Marinated Mushrooms

¾ cup salad oil
¼ cup olive oil
½ cup **MINUTE MAID® 100% Pure Lemon Juice**
1 medium onion (chopped fine)
1 tsp. salt
¼ tsp. pepper
3 bay leaves
1 tsp. chopped parsley
1½ cups small fresh tiny mushrooms or 3 cans (4 oz.) button mushrooms

Mix all ingredients except mushrooms in a jar with screw top. Shake well. Add mushrooms. Let stand 12 hours or more.

Crisco® OIL
Marinated Mushrooms

Add **2 pounds very small mushrooms** to Mild Garlic Marinade*. Marinate for several days in refrigerator. Stir or shake occasionally. Marinated mushrooms may be used as an appetizer, added to salads, or used as a garnish. Use Marinade as a salad dressing on **fresh crisp greens.**

*Mild Garlic Marinade

¼ cup **CRISCO® Oil**
3 tablespoons wine vinegar
⅓ cup tomato juice
1 teaspoon salt
1 teaspoon paprika
½ teaspoon black pepper
2 cloves garlic

Combine all ingredients in a screw-top jar and chill for several days in refrigerator. Remove garlic cloves and shake well before using. *About ¾ cup*

Mazola®
Marinated Artichoke Hearts

2 packages (9 oz. each) frozen artichoke hearts
¾ cup **MAZOLA® Corn Oil**
⅓ cup tarragon vinegar
2 tablespoons finely chopped parsley
1 tablespoon finely chopped onion
1 teaspoon dry mustard
½ teaspoon salt
¼ teaspoon pepper
1 clove garlic, minced

Cook artichoke hearts according to package directions for minimum cooking period or just until tender crisp. Drain thoroughly. Mix together remaining ingredients. Pour over artichoke hearts; cover; chill overnight. Serve cold or heat artichoke hearts in marinade in 3-quart saucepan just until heated. Spoon into fondue pot or chafing dish. Hold over low heat during serving period.
Makes about 60 appetizer pieces

Shrimp Teriyaki *(top)*, Chinese Barbecued Pork *(bottom)*
Kikkoman *(Kikkoman International)*

Empañada Grande
The Christian Brothers® *(Fromm and Sichel, Inc.)*

Hors d'Oeuvres Platter *(left)*, Instant Canapés *(right)*
Finlandia® Vodka *(The Buckingham Corp.)*

Hot Bean Dip *(top)*, Spinach Balls *(bottom)*
Van Camp's®, Stokely's®
(Stokely-Van Camp, Inc.)

Corned Beef Cheese Ball
Libby's® *(Libby, McNeill & Libby, Inc.)*

Bertolli® Stuffed Artichokes
(Bertolli U.S.A.)

Appetizer Franks With Mustard Sauce
Wilson® *(Wilson Foods Corporation)*

Wheat Germ Egg Rolls
Kretschmer *(International Multifoods)*

Lipton® California Dip
(Thomas J. Lipton, Inc.)

Scallops en Brochette
High Liner® *(National Sea Products Ltd.)*

Dorman's® Muenster Mousse
(N. Dorman & Company)

Danish Camembert Cheese Fondue
(Denmark Cheese Association)

Doused Shrimp
Lea & Perrins *(Lea & Perrins, Inc.)*

Ham Sticks With Yogurt Dill Dip, Sliced Meat Roll-Ups, Appetizer Wedges, Party Pinwheels
Oscar Mayer *(Oscar Mayer Foods Corp.)*

Panzarotti
Chef Boy-Ar-Dee® *(American Home Foods)*

Cheese Fondue
Bolla *(The Jos. Garneau Co.)*

Quick Draw Dip
Wolf® *(Wolf Brand Products)*

Barbecued Miniature Meatballs *(top)*,
French's® Stuffed Mushrooms *(bottom)*
(R. T. French Company)

Milwaukee Salami Cups
Veg-All® *(The Larsen Company)*

Deviled Eggs With Crab
(National Marine Fisheries Service)

Appetizer Chicken Mole *(left)*, Shrimp Turnovers *(center)*, Dunphy's Stuffed Mushrooms *(right)*
Metaxa®, **Planters®**, **Droste®**, **Dunphy's** *(Julius Wile Sons & Co.)*

Pickle Pinwheels
Heinz *(Heinz U.S.A.)*

Marinated Fresh Vegetables
Claussen *(Oscar Mayer Foods Corp.)*

Stack-Up Wedges
Eckrich® *(Peter Eckrich & Sons, Inc.)*

Seasoned Fish Dip
(Florida Department of Natural Resources)

Nacho Franks
(National Hot Dog & Sausage Council)

Rock Lobster in Aspic for a Buffet *(left)*, Rock Lobster Petites With Caper Mayonnaise *(right)*
South African Rock Lobster *(South African Rock Lobster Service Corporation)*

Oriental Almonds *(top)*, Almond Sausage Cheese Tarts *(center)*, Curried Almond Chicken Balls *(bottom)*
Blue Diamond® *(California Almond Growers Exchange)*

Fresh Vegetable Marinade
Campbell's *(Campbell Soup Company)*

Holiday-Sausage Stroganoff Dip
Jimmy Dean® *(Jimmy Dean Meat Company, Inc.)*

Buddig Pin Wheels *(top)*, **Buddig** Stuffed Celery *(center)*,
Piccalitoes *(bottom)*
(Carl Buddig & Company)

Sweet-Sour Dip
Jeno's® *(Jeno's)*

Heavenly Ham Dip in a Bread Bowl
Bridgford *(Bridgford Foods Corporation)*

Cheesy Walnut Pinwheels *(left)*, Chili-Cheese Rounds *(right)*
Bisquick® *(General Mills, Inc.)*

Fishermen's Best Spread
Knox®, **Wish-Bone**® *(Thomas J. Lipton, Inc.)*

Slender Sliced Beef Party Dip
Eckrich® *(Peter Eckrich & Sons, Inc.)*

Bantry Bay Shrimp Toast
Irish Mist® *(Heublein Inc.)*

Fruit Cheese Log
Del Monte *(Del Monte Corp.)*

Original Ranch® Dip
Hidden Valley Ranch® *(The Clorox Company)*

Mexican Tarts
3-Minute Brand®, Harvest Brand®
(National Oats Company, Inc.)

Hot Beef 'n Frank Tidbits
Lea & Perrins *(Lea & Perrins, Inc.)*

Jimmy Dean® Nachos
(Jimmy Dean Meat Company, Inc.)

Little Links in Sauce
Oscar Mayer (*Oscar Mayer Foods Corp.*)

Angostura® Vegetable Dip
(*A-W Brands, Inc.*)

Kabobs *(top)*, Sausage Smorgasbord of Snacks *(bottom)*
Hillshire Farm® *(Kahn's and Company)*

Continental Snacks *(top)*, Danish 'n Eggs *(bottom)*
Sara Lee *(Kitchens of Sara Lee)*

Sweet and Sour Meatballs
Wolff's® *(The Birkett Mills)*

Double Decker Pizza
Rhodes™ *(Dakota Bake-N-Serv, Inc.)*

46

Blushing Bagelette, Tuna Toppers, Beefy Bagelette
Lender's ® *(Lender's Bagel Bakery, Inc.)*

Praline® Popcorn Crunch
(Hiram Walker Inc.)

Continental Sausage Sampler
Hillshire Farm® *(Kahn's and Company)*

Cheese 'n Comfort
Southern Comfort® *(Southern Comfort Corp.)*

(clockwise from top) Pepperoni 'n Cheese Crescents, Cheezy Tater Crescent Snacks, Nutty Garlic Snacks, Crescent-Easy Pretzels
Hungry Jack®, **Pillsbury**, **Cheez Whiz**, **Kraft**, **Parkay**
(The Pillsbury Company)

Celtic Oysters Rockefeller
Irish Mist® *(Heublein Inc.)*

Teriyaki Meat Sticks *(left)*, Menehune Chicken *(right)*
Kikkoman *(Kikkoman International)*

Jif
Tuna Nibblers

1 6½- or 7-ounce can tuna, drained and flaked
1 hard-cooked egg, mashed
¼ cup JIF® Creamy Peanut Butter
2 tablespoons mayonnaise or salad dressing
1 tablespoon lemon juice
1 tablespoon diced dill pickle
1 tablespoon pickle juice
Dash bottled hot pepper sauce
Saltines or snack crackers
Sliced pimiento-stuffed olives

Combine tuna, egg, JIF®, mayonnaise or salad dressing, lemon juice, diced pickle, pickle juice, and hot pepper sauce. Blend thoroughly. Spread mixture on saltines or snack crackers; top each with an olive slice.   *Makes about 25*

VARIATION:

Beef Nibblers

Substitute one 6-ounce package *smoked pressed beef*, finely snipped, for the tuna.

Anchovy Canapé

HI HO CRACKERS®
Anchovy paste
Thinly sliced fresh mushrooms
Lemon juice
Anchovy filets
Minced chives

Spread crackers with layer of anchovy paste. Add a layer of mushrooms that have been marinated in lemon juice. Place anchovy filet on top. Sprinkle with chives. Serve on HI HO CRACKERS®.

Canapé a la Cavalier

Upon white bread, cut in fancy shapes, spread a mixture of equal parts of AMBER BRAND Deviled SMITHFIELD Ham and PHILADELPHIA BRAND Cream Cheese. Decorate with slices of stuffed green olives.

Celery and Eggs

2 cups finely chopped celery with leaves
6 hard-boiled eggs, chopped
3 tablespoons oil
1 teaspoon salt
¼ teaspoon pepper
1 small onion, chopped
Paprika
SUNSHINE® Crackers

Combine first six ingredients, and mix. Chill and serve, topped with paprika, on assorted SUNSHINE® Crackers.

Liverwurst Smorrebrod

1 can (4¾ ounces) UNDERWOOD® Liverwurst Spread
2 tablespoons mayonnaise
12 slices party rye bread
24 slices cherry tomato
12 slices cucumber
2 tablespoons chopped scallion

In a bowl, mix liverwurst spread and mayonnaise. Spread on party rye slices. Top with slices of cherry tomato, cucumber and chopped scallion.   *Makes 12 snacks*

Danish Chipwich

1⅓ cups crab meat (flaked fine)
¼ cup mayonnaise
¼ cup finely chopped pickled onions
Hard cooked egg
Green pepper
Olives
Large JAYS Potato Chips

Stir mayonnaise and onions into crab meat. Spread on large crisp Potato Chips and garnish with olive slices or green pepper strips and hard cooked egg slices.

Water Chestnut Canapés

1 package FRITO-LAY® Brand Garlic and Onion Dip Mix
1 3-ounce package cream cheese, softened
¼ cup milk
¼ cup diced green pepper
¼ cup diced pimiento
¼ cup chopped slivered almonds
½ cup diced cooked chicken or turkey breasts
1 8-ounce can whole water chestnuts

Drain chestnuts and slice. Combine FRITO-LAY® Brand Garlic and Onion Dip Mix, cream cheese and milk. Add pepper, pimiento, almonds, chicken or turkey. Mix well. Place mounds of mixture on top of each chestnut slice. Chill and serve cold.
                    Makes 30 appetizers

Lite-line
Salmon Canapés
(Low Calorie)

½ cup canned red salmon, drained and flaked
1 tablespoon low calorie mayonnaise
⅛ teaspoon dill weed
12 OLD LONDON® Melba Rounds
3 slices BORDEN® LITE-LINE® Pasteurized Process Cheese Product, quartered
12 thin slices cucumber
Parsley

In small bowl, combine salmon, mayonnaise and dill; mix well. On top of each Melba round, place a cheese product piece, a
                    (Continued)

(Continued)
cucumber slice, 2 teaspoons salmon mixture and parsley. Serve immediately. Refrigerate leftovers. *Makes 12 snacks*

Calories: Prepared as directed, provides approximately 440 or 36 per snack. (Values by product analyses and recipe calculations.)

Caviar Cucumber Rounds

1 pkg. (3 oz.) cream cheese, softened
2 tsp. milk
22 ⅓-inch thick slices pared cucumber (from 2 small cucumbers)
3 Tbsp. (1½ oz.) ROMANOFF® Caviar*
Lemon juice
22 small cocktail onions

Blend cream cheese and milk. Spread on cucumbers. Spoon a little caviar in center of each. (Use a quarter-teaspoon measure or a small melon baller.) Sprinkle with lemon juice. Drain onions on paper towel. Place one on each round, in center of caviar.

Makes 22

*ROMANOFF® Red Lumpfish or Salmon Caviar suggested.

ARMOUR®
Creamy Beef Roll-Ups

1 8-oz. pkg. cream cheese, softened
2 Tbsp. prepared horseradish
1 2½-oz. jar ARMOUR STAR® Sliced Dried Beef, rinsed

Combine cream cheese and horseradish. Spread mixture on double dried beef slices; roll up. Chill. *10 to 12 appetizers*

VARIATION:

Substitute ¼ cup chopped green onions for horseradish.

Campbell's
Fresh Vegetable Marinade

1 can (10¾ ounces) CAMPBELL'S Condensed Chicken Broth
¼ cup vinegar
2 tablespoons salad oil
2 tablespoons dry vermouth
1 package (about 0.9 ounces) mild Italian salad dressing mix
2 cups thinly sliced sweet potatoes
2 cups thinly sliced zucchini squash
1 cup thinly sliced broccoli flowerets
1 cup thinly sliced cauliflowerets
1 cup thinly sliced fresh mushrooms
1 cup cherry tomatoes cut in half

To make marinade, combine broth, vinegar, oil, vermouth and salad dressing mix. Arrange vegetables in shallow dish; pour marinade over vegetables. Cover. Chill 6 hours or more; stir occasionally. With slotted spoon, arrange vegetables on platter.

Makes about 7 cups

DEMING'S
Salmon Antipasto

15½ oz. can DEMING'S Red Sockeye Salmon*
2 stalks celery, sliced into 1 in. pieces
2 carrots sliced lengthwise into 3 in. sticks
2-3 cups cauliflower flowerets
2-3 cups broccoli flowerets
¼ pound fresh mushrooms, cleaned and sliced
10 oz. can artichoke hearts, drained and halved
16 oz. can whole green beans, drained
16 oz. bottle Italian Dressing & Marinade
Cherry tomatoes
Stuffed or ripe olives
Crisp crackers or toast points

Drain salmon and break into bite size pieces in small bowl. Sprinkle with 3 Tbsp. dressing; cover and chill for 2 hrs. Cook celery, carrots, cauliflower, and broccoli in small amount of water until tender-crisp. Drain and place in shallow container with mushrooms, artichoke hearts and green beans. Pour remaining dressing over all until vegetables are well coated; cover and chill. When ready to serve, remove vegetables and salmon from marinade and arrange attractively on a platter with cherry tomatoes, olives and crisp crackers or toast points. *Serves 10-12*

*DOUBLE Q, GILLNETTERSBEST or HUMPTY DUMPTY Salmon may be substituted.

Antipasto

The antipasto tray begins the meal and may have up to ten choices of meat, cheese, fish and vegetables. The presentation of the food is important. Use contrast in color, shape, taste and texture. Foods should be arranged in groupings of shapes, such as wedges and strips, rounds and triangles.

An excellent antipasto would include marinated vegetables, tuna in oil, salami, provolone cheese, green and black olives and Eggplant Caponata. Always serve the antipasto with cruets of BERTOLLI® Olive Oil and BERTOLLI® Red Wine Vinegar.

Eggplant Caponata

1 large eggplant, cut into ¾-inch cubes
1½ tablespoons salt
1 cup finely chopped celery
1 cup finely chopped onion
2 cloves garlic, minced
½ cup BERTOLLI® Olive Oil
1¼ cups BERTOLLI® Spaghetti Sauce
¼ cup pimiento-stuffed olives, cut into fourths
3 tablespoons pine nuts
1½ tablespoons drained capers
3 anchovies, minced
2 tablespoons BERTOLLI® Red Wine Vinegar
2 teaspoons sugar
⅛ teaspoon crushed red pepper

Sprinkle eggplant with salt; let stand 30 minutes. Rinse; pat dry. Sauté eggplant, celery, onion and garlic in oil in Dutch oven until eggplant is browned, about 10 minutes. Stir in remaining ingredients; heat to boiling. Reduce heat; simmer 15 minutes. Spoon into bowl; refrigerate until cold.

Marinated Cauliflower

½ cup **HEINZ Salad or Wine Vinegar**
¼ cup salad oil
1 clove garlic, minced
1 teaspoon salt
Dash pepper
Dash paprika
1 small head cauliflower (about 1½ pounds), cut into bite-size pieces
1 small onion, thinly sliced
2 tablespoons chopped green pepper
1 tablespoon pimiento strips

Combine first 6 ingredients in jar; cover; shake well. In bowl, combine cauliflower and remaining ingredients. Pour marinade over vegetables. Cover; refrigerate overnight, stirring occasionally. Serve as a relish, appetizer or salad.

Makes about 4 cups

Marinated Fresh Vegetables

Heat juice from 1 jar **CLAUSSEN Kosher Pickles** (about 2 cups). Arrange fresh vegetables—cherry tomatoes, celery, carrots, cauliflower and broccoli in empty pickle jar. Pour heated juice over vegetables and replace lid. Refrigerate vegetables 24 hours before serving.

PROGRESSO
QUALITY ITALIAN FOODS

Tuna and Fried Peppers
(Tonno e Peperoni Fritte)

1 jar (6 oz.) sweet fried peppers and onions
1 can (7 oz.) tuna, drained and flaked
3 tablespoons finely chopped onion
3 tablespoons chopped parsley
2 teaspoons **PROGRESSO Wine Vinegar**
⅛ teaspoon ground black pepper
Lettuce leaves

In a medium bowl combine all ingredients except lettuce. Arrange lettuce leaves on a platter to form a cup; fill with tuna and pepper mixture. Serve with oil cured olives, if desired.

Yield: 8 appetizer portions

Anchovy and Sweet Pepper

1 flat can of anchovies
2 sweet red peppers (pimientos)
8 Tbsp. of **FILIPPO BERIO Olive Oil**
1½ Tbsp. of **FILIPPO BERIO Wine Vinegar**

Cut pimiento into slices about ½-inch wide and 3-inches long. Take out filets of anchovies from can and drain off the oil. Place one anchovy on each strip of pimiento, rolling them together into a circle and piercing them with a toothpick to hold them firm. Place them in a serving dish. Mix the **FILIPPO BERIO Olive Oil** and **Wine Vinegar** thoroughly and pour over pimiento and anchovy rolls. Serve with Melba crackers.

FINLANDIA
Vodka

Hors d'Oeuvres Platter

Arrange neatly: salami slices, rolled-up slices of cooked ham, drained tuna chunks speared on toothpicks, cheese cubes on toothpicks, cherry tomatoes, drained sardines on toothpicks, pickle slices, walnut halves sandwiched together with blue cheese spread, hard-cooked egg halves spread with mayonnaise and topped with 2 rolled drained anchovies and 3 capers. Serve with **FINLANDIA® Vodka**.

SWEET 'N LOW BRAND

Mock Herring
(Low Calorie/Low Fat)

2 medium onions, sliced
2 stalks celery, cut into 1-inch pieces
1 small eggplant, peeled and cut into long strips, 1-inch wide
1 cup plain low-fat yogurt
1 tablespoon lemon juice
1 packet **SWEET 'N LOW®**
¼ teaspoon salt
⅛ teaspoon ground cloves
1 bay leaf

Steam onions and celery in vegetable steamer over boiling water 5 to 6 minutes. Add eggplant and steam about 5 minutes, or until soft but not mushy. Remove vegetables to bowl and set aside to cool. In separate bowl, combine remaining ingredients; mix gently with cooled vegetables. Remove bay leaf. Chill thoroughly. Serve on whole-grain bread or crackers. *About 3½ cups*

Per Serving (⅓ cup): Calories: 30; Fat: 1g

Gallo® Salame and Tropical Fruit Tray

24 slices **GALLO® Italian Dry Salame**
8 oz. cream cheese, at room temperature
⅓ cup sour cream
2 Tbsp. each chopped shallots or green onions and chopped parsley
Salt and pepper to taste
Dash **TABASCO® Sauce**
1 large pineapple
2 papaya
1 basket of strawberries
4 bananas
1 lime, cut in wedges

Beat until blended cream cheese, sour cream, shallots, parsley, salt and pepper to taste, and **TABASCO®**. Spread spoonful on one side of each **GALLO® Salame** slice and roll to form cone shapes. Skewer with toothpicks and place at end of tray. Peel and slice pineapple (into spears), papaya, and banana (diagonally). Clean strawberries. Arrange fruits on the tray with **GALLO® Italian Dry Salame**. Garnish with lime wedges. *Serves 6 to 8*

Deviled Eggs Deluxe
Bacon

6 hard-cooked eggs*
2 tablespoons mayonnaise or salad dressing
2 tablespoons cooked, drained and crumbled bacon
1 teaspoon Worcestershire sauce
¼ teaspoon celery seed

Cut eggs in half lengthwise. Remove yolks; mash with fork. Add remaining ingredients; mix until blended. Refill egg whites using approx. 1 tablespoon mixture per egg half; chill.

Makes 12 deviled halves

Ham

6 hard-cooked eggs*
¼ cup finely minced ham
3½-4 tablespoons mayonnaise or salad dressing
¼ teaspoon dill weed

Cut eggs in half lengthwise. Remove yolks; mash with fork. Add remaining ingredients; mix until blended. Refill egg whites using approx. 1 tablespoon mixture per egg half; chill.

Makes 12 deviled halves

Tuna

6 hard-cooked eggs*
¼ cup drained, flaked tuna
3½-4 tablespoons dairy sour cream
¼-½ teaspoon curry powder

Cut eggs in half lengthwise. Remove yolks; mash with fork. Add remaining ingredients; mix until blended. Refill egg whites using approx. 1 tablespoon mixture per egg half; chill.

Makes 12 deviled halves

O'Brien

6 hard-cooked eggs*
2 tablespoons finely chopped green pepper
1½-2 tablespoons dairy sour cream
1 teaspoon finely chopped pimiento
½ teaspoon instant minced onion

Cut eggs in half lengthwise. Remove yolks; mash with fork. Add remaining ingredients; mix until blended. Refill egg whites using approx. 1 tablespoon mixture per egg half; chill.

Makes 12 deviled halves

*Hard-Cooked Eggs

Eggs
Water

Cover eggs in pan with enough water to come at least 1 inch above eggs. Cover; bring rapidly just to boiling. Turn off heat; if necessary remove pan from unit to prevent further boiling. Cover; let stand in hot water 15 minutes for large eggs—adjust time up or down accordingly for other sizes. Cool eggs immediately and thoroughly in cold water—shells are easier to remove and dark surface is prevented on yolks. To remove shell: Crackle shell by tapping gently all over. Roll egg between hands to loosen shell; then peel, starting at large end. Holding egg under running cold water or dipping in bowl of water helps to ease off shell.

Favorite recipe from the **American Egg Board**

Morton Salt
Olive Deviled Eggs

2 dozen eggs, hard-cooked
⅔ cup mayonnaise
¼ cup minced pimiento-stuffed green olives
1 teaspoon oregano
½ teaspoon **MORTON Table Salt**
¼ teaspoon black pepper
¼ teaspoon garlic powder
Lettuce leaves

Day before serving or early in day: Cut hard-cooked eggs in half lengthwise. Remove yolks to small mixing bowl; mash. Add remaining ingredients except lettuce leaves; mix well. Fill whites with yolk mixture. Cover and refrigerate.

Just before serving: Place eggs on lettuce-lined platter.

Makes 48

Deviled Eggs With Crab

1 package (6 ounces) snow crab or other crabmeat, frozen or 1 can (6½ ounces) crabmeat
6 hard-cooked eggs
3 tablespoons finely chopped celery
4 heaping tablespoons mayonnaise
1 teaspoon dry mustard
¼ teaspoon salt
Dash pepper
1 teaspoon finely chopped parsley
⅛ teaspoon oregano
⅛ teaspoon garlic powder
4 drops Worcestershire sauce

Thaw crabmeat if frozen. Drain canned crabmeat. Remove any remaining shell or cartilage. Peel eggs and cut in half lengthwise. Remove yolks, put in bowl and mash well. Add celery, mayonnaise and seasonings. Add crabmeat and mix well. Stuff egg whites with yolk mixture. Chill before serving.

Makes 1 dozen

Favorite recipe from the **National Marine Fisheries Service**

Deviled Eggs au Poulet
(Low Calorie)

6 hard-cooked eggs
1 can (5 ounces) SWANSON Chunk Style Mixin' Chicken
3 tablespoons imitation mayonnaise
1 tablespoon finely chopped celery
1 tablespoon finely chopped onion
1 tablespoon Dijon mustard
1 tablespoon sweet pickle relish

Cut eggs in half lengthwise. Scoop out yolks; mash. Stir in remaining ingredients. Stuff into egg whites; sprinkle with paprika. Chill.
Makes 12 deviled eggs

Calories: about 70 each

Pimiento Deviled Eggs

Drain 1 (2-ounce) jar **DROMEDARY Sliced Pimientos**. Finely chop enough to make 1 tablespoon chopped. Cut 6 hard-cooked eggs in half lengthwise. Remove yolks and mash. Combine with 2 tablespoons mayonnaise, the chopped pimiento, 2 teaspoons cider vinegar and ⅛ teaspoon salt. Stuff egg whites and garnish with remaining sliced pimientos. *Makes 12*

San Giorgio®
Tubettini Deviled Eggs

¼ cup (2 ounces) **SAN GIORGIO® Tubettini**, uncooked
6 hard-cooked eggs
⅓ cup cottage cheese
2 teaspoons milk
2 teaspoons prepared mustard
2 tablespoons sweet pickle relish or chopped pickle

Cook Tubettini according to package directions; drain well. Cool. (Rinse with cold water to cool quickly; drain well.)

Slice eggs in half; remove yolks. Combine yolks, cottage cheese, milk, mustard and relish or chopped pickle; blend well by hand or process in blender or food processor until smooth. Stir in cooled Tubettini; fill egg whites with macaroni mixture. Chill.

12 eggs

Cottage Cheese Nut Ring

2 pounds cottage cheese
½ cup **PLANTERS® Dry Roasted Mixed Nuts**
1 teaspoon curry powder

Combine cottage cheese, **PLANTERS® Dry Roasted Mixed Nuts** and curry powder; beat until thoroughly blended. Place cheese mixture in a greased 9-inch ring mold. Chill until firm (about 2 hours). Unmold and serve with sliced fresh fruit.

Makes 6 servings

Fruit Cheese Log

½ cup **DEL MONTE Dried Apricots**
1 cup water
1 lb. Monterey Jack cheese, shredded
1 pkg. (8 oz.) cream cheese, softened
⅓ cup milk*
1 tsp. poppy seed
½ tsp. seasoned salt
⅓ cup **DEL MONTE Golden Seedless Raisins**
¼ cup pitted dates, snipped
¾ cup chopped walnuts
Crackers

Soak apricots in water two hours; drain and chop. Blend cheeses. Add milk, poppy seed and salt; mix well. Fold in fruit; mix well. Turn out on foil; shape into log-type roll. Wrap securely in foil; chill until firm. Roll in nuts before serving. Serve with crackers.

1 log (approximately 2 lbs.)

*VARIATION:

Substitute ⅓ cup sherry for milk.

Almond Cheese Pinecone

2 packages (8 ounces *each*) cream cheese, softened
2 jars (5 ounces *each*) pasteurized process cheese spread with pimiento
½ pound blue cheese, crumbled
¼ cup minced green onion
½ teaspoon Worcestershire sauce
2 cups **BLUE DIAMOND® Blanched Whole Almonds**, toasted
Pine sprigs for garnish
Crackers

In large bowl with mixer at medium speed, beat cream cheese, cheese spread with pimiento and blue cheese until smooth. With spoon, stir in green onions and Worcestershire sauce. Cover and refrigerate about one hour.

On work surface, with hands, shape cheese mixture into shape of large pinecone. Arrange on wooden board. Beginning at narrow end of cone, carefully press almonds about ¼ inch deep into cheese mixture in rows, making sure that pointed end of each almond extends at a slight angle. Continue pressing almonds into cheese mixture in rows, with rows slightly overlapping, until all cheese is covered. Garnish pinecone with pine sprigs. Serve with crackers. *Makes about 25 servings*

"Philly" Cheese Bell

1 8-oz. pkg. **CRACKER BARREL Brand Sharp Cheddar Flavor Cold Pack Cheese Food**
1 8-oz. pkg. **PHILADELPHIA BRAND Cream Cheese**
PARKAY Margarine
2 teaspoons chopped pimiento
2 teaspoons chopped green pepper
2 teaspoons chopped onion
1 teaspoon Worcestershire sauce
½ teaspoon lemon juice

Combine cold pack cheese food, softened cream cheese and 2 tablespoons margarine; mix until well blended. Add remaining ingredients; mix well. Mold into bell shapes, using the cold pack container coated with margarine or lined with plastic wrap. Chill until firm; unmold. Garnish with chopped parsley and pimiento strips, if desired. *2 bells*

Cheese Appetizer Roll

2 cups (½ pound) shredded Cheddar cheese
2 hard-cooked eggs, finely chopped
2 tablespoons chopped pimiento
1 tablespoon Worcestershire sauce
Few drops hot pepper sauce
½ cup chopped **FISHER®'S Salted Soybeans**
⅓ cup dairy sour cream
½ teaspoon salt
Chopped **FISHER®'S Salted Pecans**

Combine ingredients except chopped soybeans; chill several hours. Form into a roll about 2 inches in diameter. Roll in chopped soybeans. Wrap in foil or waxed paper; chill several hours or overnight. To serve, cut into thin slices and place on crackers. *About 2 Dozen*

QUAKER

Cheese Ball

Two 8-oz. pkg. cream cheese, softened
2 cups (8 oz.) shredded Swiss cheese
One 8-oz. can crushed pineapple, well drained
3 crisply cooked bacon slices, crumbled
¼ cup finely chopped celery
1 teaspoon Worcestershire sauce
¼ teaspoon salt
1 cup QUAKER® 100% Natural Cereal, coarsely
    crushed

Beat together cream cheese and Swiss cheese, mixing until well
blended. Stir in pineapple, bacon, celery, Worcestershire sauce
and salt; mix well. Chill until firm. Shape to form 1 large or 2
small balls; chill. Just before serving, roll ball in cereal, coating
well. Serve with crackers or raw vegetables, as desired.

Makes about 12 servings

Libby's
Libby's
Libby's

Corned Beef Cheese Ball

1 can (12 oz.) LIBBY'S® Corned Beef
1 container (8 oz.) small-curd cottage cheese
¼ cup sliced scallions
¼ cup minced green pepper
2 tablespoons minced parsley
1 tablespoon prepared horseradish
¼ teaspoon salt
⅛ teaspoon TABASCO®
⅛ teaspoon garlic powder
1 package (8 oz.) cream cheese, softened
Assorted crackers, thick cucumber slices, celery stalks
Parsley sprigs, garnish

Crumble corned beef into a medium bowl. Add cottage cheese,
scallions, green pepper, parsley and seasonings; mix thoroughly.
Chill several hours to blend flavors and to firm mixture. Remove
mixture from bowl and shape into a ball. Spread cream cheese
evenly over ball. Wrap in plastic wrap and refrigerate until ready
to pack. Serve on a cheese board or tray with assorted crackers and
thick cucumber slices for spreading, celery stalks for stuffing.
Garnish with parsley sprigs if desired.

Chippy Cheese Ball

1 pound sharp Cheddar cheese, grated
¼ pound ROQUEFORT Cheese, crumbled
½ pound cream cheese
2 tablespoons grated onion
2 teaspoons Worcestershire sauce
¼ teaspoon cayenne pepper
1¼ cups crushed LAY'S® Brand Sour Cream & Onion
    Flavored Potato Chips

Have cheese at room temperature. Blend well with mixer or pastry
blender. Add Worcestershire sauce, onion, pepper, and ¼ cup of

the crushed LAY'S® Brand Sour Cream & Onion Flavored
Potato Chips. Shape into ball and roll in remaining LAY'S®
Brand Sour Cream & Onion Flavored Potato Chips until
completely covered. Chill well. (This cheese ball will freeze well.)

Hormel

Almond Pepperoni
Cheese Ball

8 oz. cream cheese
10 oz. Cheddar cheese spread
2 Tbsp. sour cream
18 slices HORMEL Pepperoni
Sliced almonds for garnish

Mix together softened cream cheese, Cheddar spread and sour
cream. On waxed paper form mixture into a ball. Add in 12 slices
of pepperoni chopped into eighths. Garnish with whole pepperoni
slices and almonds thrust into ball.

FINLANDIA
IMPORTED
SWISS CHEESE

Cocktail Party Ball

1 pound shredded FINLANDIA Swiss
¼ pound ROQUEFORT Cheese, crumbled
1 package (8 ounces) cream cheese
1 tablespoon grated onion
2 teaspoons Worcestershire sauce
Dash cayenne pepper
½ cup chopped toasted pecans
½ cup finely chopped parsley

Bring cheeses to room temperature. Place in electric mixer and
blend well. Add onion, Worcestershire sauce and cayenne pepper.
Shape into ball, wrap in waxed paper or plastic wrap. Chill several
hours. Just before serving combine pecans and parsley. Roll ball in
mixture. Serve with crackers. *Makes 8 to 10 servings*

Wyler's®

Chicken Cheese Ball

1 (8-ounce) package cream cheese, softened
½ cup finely chopped cooked chicken
2 tablespoons chopped pimiento
1 teaspoon WYLER'S® Chicken-Flavor Instant
    Bouillon
½ cup coarsely chopped nuts or sunflower seeds
OLD LONDON® Melba Rounds

In small bowl, combine all ingredients except nuts and Melba
rounds; mix well. Shape into a ball; roll in nuts to coat. Chill.
Garnish as desired. Serve with Melba rounds. Refrigerate
leftovers.

Smoky Pimiento Cheese Ball

One 8-oz. container **WISPRIDE Hickory Smoked Cold Pack Cheese Food**, softened
One 8-oz. package cream cheese, softened
¼ cup bacon crumbs (4 strips, cooked and crumbled)
1 tablespoon chopped pimiento
1 teaspoon Worcestershire sauce
½ teaspoon lemon juice
½ cup finely chopped pecans

In small bowl, combine **WISPRIDE** and cream cheese; beat until smooth and creamy. Add bacon, pimiento, Worcestershire sauce and lemon juice; mix well. Chill in refrigerator until pliable (about 1 hour). With spatula or wooden spoon, shape into a ball. Roll in pecans.
Makes one cheese ball

Olive-Cheese Balls

Roll stuffed olives in softened cream cheese, then in chopped pecans.

Favorite recipe from the **National Pecan Marketing Council**

Cheese Tempters

4 oz. pkg. **SARGENTO Shredded Natural Cheddar Cheese**
¼ cup butter or margarine (room temperature)
½ cup sifted flour
¼ tsp. salt
¼ cup corn flakes
Paprika

Combine cheese and butter until well blended. Add flour and salt and mix. Add corn flakes and mix with hands until mixture holds together. Pinch off small amount and roll into a ball. Place balls on ungreased baking sheet 2″ apart. Sprinkle with paprika and bake at 400° F. for 20 minutes.

Roquefort Cocktail Balls

¼ lb. **ROQUEFORT Cheese**
1 tablespoon chopped celery
1 tablespoon chopped scallions
½ cup sour cream
Paprika

In an electric blender or with a fork, blend **ROQUEFORT Cheese**, celery, scallions and sour cream. Shape into small balls, the size of a walnut, and sprinkle with paprika. Chill.
Makes about 2 dozen balls

Favorite recipe from the **Roquefort Association, Inc.**

Quick & Easy Appetizers

Party Pinwheels
(Low Calorie)

Spread 1 pkg. (8 oz.) **OSCAR MAYER 95% Fat-Free Luxury Loaf** with 3 ounces imitation cream cheese. Roll first slice, join meat edges to start second slice, and continue to roll 4 slices into log. Repeat using remaining 4 slices. Wrap and chill; cut into ¼-inch slices.
Makes 32 pinwheels

Calories: 15 each

Smoke Flavor Cheese and Bacon Pinwheels

Trim the brown crust from an unsliced loaf of white bread. Slice bread lengthwise in ¼-inch strips.
Season a package of Cream Cheese with ½ teaspoon of **FIGARO Barbecue Smoke**; add celery salt and garlic salt to taste. Blend well.
Spread mixture on bread strips; roll them like a jelly roll. Chill, then cut into one-inch slices. Surround each slice with a narrow strip of thin bacon. Toast in moderate oven until bacon is crisp.

Buddig Pin Wheels

1 3-ounce package cream cheese, softened
1 tablespoon grated onion
1 teaspoon horseradish
Dash Worcestershire sauce
1 package **BUDDIG Smoked Sliced Beef** or **Ham**

Blend cream cheese, onion, horseradish and Worcestershire sauce until of spreading consistency. Carefully separate slices of **BUDDIG Beef** or **Ham** and spread with cheese mixture. Roll as for jelly roll and fasten with toothpicks. Chill. Just before serving, slice into ½-inch slices.

ECKRICH®

Famous Eckrich® Slender Sliced Pinwheels

Stack three slices of your favorite **ECKRICH® Slender Sliced Meat**. Spread softened cream cheese on the top slice and roll, jelly roll fashion. Chill until cheese is firm. Then place five toothpicks along loose edge of each roll and cut between the picks with a very sharp knife.

One package Slender Sliced Meats
will make about 15 pinwheels

Ribbon Cubes

Spread 1 pkg. (8 oz.) **OSCAR MAYER Chopped Ham** and 2 slices very thin square pumpernickel bread with 1 pkg. (3 oz.) cream cheese and chives. Stack in following order: 3 slices ham, one slice bread, 2 slices ham, one slice bread, 3 slices ham. Wrap tightly and chill. Cut into cubes. Use picks to serve.

Makes 16

Wrap-Ups

Take **OSCAR MAYER Bologna** or other sliced cold meats and wrap around dill pickles, cheese, fruit, chopped eggs, or fresh vegetables. Fasten with a pick. Chill until ready to serve.

Pickle Pinwheels

Cold cuts, thinly sliced (salami, bologna, ham)
HEINZ Sweet Gherkins or **Baby Dills** (whole), **HEINZ Sweet** or **Dill Pickles** (Spears)
Cheese, at room temperature for ease in spreading and rolling (cream cheese, cheese spreads, sliced mozzarella, process cheese slices)

Select thin, straight pickles and set out on paper towel. Spread cream cheese or cheese spread on a slice of meat. Cover with a slice of cheese or another slice of meat. Spread top slice with cream cheese or cheese spread. Lay pickle at edge; roll jelly-roll fashion. Wrap each roll tightly in plastic film; chill several hours or overnight. Slice rolls crosswise into ¼ inch rounds. Arrange pinwheels on platter. Serve with assorted crackers.

Stack-Up Wedges

6 slices ECKRICH® Cooked Salami*
Softened cream cheese or cheese spread
¼ cup finely-chopped walnuts

Spread softened cream cheese (or your favorite cheese spread) evenly over meat slices. Stack slices together, with the top slice covered with cheese spread. Sprinkle top with chopped walnuts. Wrap in plastic wrap; chill well. At serving time, cut stack into pie-shaped wedges. Arrange on serving tray with assorted crackers.

Makes 16 wedges

*Or your favorite **ECKRICH®** luncheon meat.

Cucumber Hors d'Oeuvre

1. 3 oz. cream cheese—6 small cocktail onions. Put both in blender & mix well. Chill. Decorate **CALAVO®-BURNAC EUROPEAN Cucumber** slices with cheese mixture and slices of green olives, ½ of cocktail onion, small pieces of green pepper, sliced ripe olives, almonds, or pimento.
2. Top cucumber slices with Caviar.
3. Use 3″ diameter tortilla chips. Put 1 tsp. refried beans in center of tortilla rounds. Add a small square of cheese to the top & broil until cheese melts. Add a cucumber slice to the top & sprinkle with chili powder.

Appetizer Wedges
(Low Calorie)

Remove stack of meat from an 8 ounce package of **OSCAR MAYER 90% Fat-Free Beef Honey Roll**. Cut into eight pie-shaped wedges. Separate wedges into 5 slices each. Top each with an onion and secure with pick.

Makes 16 wedges

Calories: 25 each

Cream Cheese Stuffed Canadian Bacon Appetizers

1 8-oz. pkg. cream cheese, softened
2 tablespoons dry onion soup mix
1 5-oz. pkg. **COUNTRY SMOKED MEATS Canadian Bacon Slices**

Combine dry onion soup mix and cream cheese. Divide and lay filling onto center of each slice of Canadian Bacon; chill. When chilled, cut into bite size pieces and fasten with toothpicks.

Sliced Meat Roll-Ups
(Low Calorie)

Remove stack of meat from an 8 ounce package of **OSCAR MAYER 93% Fat-Free Peppered Loaf**. Cut stack in half diagonally. Wrap half slices around pickle spear, celery, carrots or other crisp vegetables. Secure with pick.

Makes 20 roll-ups

Calories: 20 each

Instant Canapés

Breads: Any sliced bread, cut into small squares, toasted. Plain crackers. Spread with any of the following:

SAVORY BUTTERS: Cream butter and blend with: **Anchovy**—½ cup butter, 2 tablespoons anchovy paste. **Chive, or Scallion or Watercress**—½ cup butter, ⅓ cup finely minced greens. **Ham**—½ cup butter, 3 tablespoons minced ham or ham spread. **Horseradish**—½ cup butter, ¼ cup grated horseradish (drain if bottled). **Lemon**—½ cup butter, 1 teaspoon grated lemon rind, 2 tablespoons fresh lemon juice.

SPREADS: Mix 3 ounces of cream cheese with 1 tablespoon sweet or sour cream. Blend with: **Chutney**—3 tablespoons finely chopped chutney. **Blue Cheese**—2 tablespoons blue cheese and ¼ teaspoon Worcestershire sauce. **Caper**—3 tablespoons drained chopped capers. **Caviar**—4 tablespoons red caviar and 1 teaspoon grated onion. **Nut**—½ cup chopped salted nuts. **Olive**—½ cup chopped green stuffed or pitted black olives.

Serve with **FINLANDIA®** Vodka.

Cracker Toppings

Ham 'n Cheese

Top **SOCIABLES Crackers** with small ham rolls and sliced olives. Garnish with **SNACK MATE Sharp Cheddar Pasteurized Process Cheese Spread**.

Harvest Squares

Top **TRISCUIT Wafers** with thin slices of red and yellow apples. Garnish with **SNACK MATE Cheese 'n Bacon Pasteurized Process Cheese Spread**.

Fruit 'n Cheese Special

Top **ESCORT Crackers** with Mandarin orange segments and halved green grapes. Garnish with **SNACK MATE American Pasteurized Process Cheese Spread**.

Shrimply Delicious

Top **Buttery Flavored Sesame Snack Crackers** with thin cucumber slices and cooked small shrimp. Garnish with **SNACK MATE Chive 'n Green Onion Pasteurized Process Cheese Spread**.

Bacon 'n Egg

Top **SESAME WHEATS Snack Crackers** with crumbled cooked bacon, chopped hard-cooked egg and parsley sprigs. Garnish with **SNACK MATE Cheddar Pasteurized Process Cheese Spread**.

Canadian Bacon Roll-Ups

¼ lb. **COUNTRY SMOKED MEATS Canadian Bacon**, sliced thin
6 green onions
1 8-oz. pkg. cream cheese

Take one slice of Canadian Bacon, lay flat and spread with cream cheese. Roll this around one green onion. Slice into ½″ pieces.
Makes about 72 Roll-Ups

Dips & Spreads

Spreads

Plowman's Cheese Spread

Beat until smooth and well blended 1 large package (8 oz.) softened cream cheese, 1½ cups shredded sharp Cheddar cheese, ¼ cup **ALMADÉN Mountain White Chablis** wine, 1 teaspoon paprika, ½ teaspoon garlic salt and a dash of cayenne. Serve the nippy cheese spread from a stoneware crock to lavish on crusty whole wheat bread or wedges of a tart apple.
Makes about 2 cups

Cheese 'n Comfort

1 Edam cheese or 8 oz. cream cheese
¼ lb. sharp Cheddar cheese
¼ lb. butter
¼ cup **SOUTHERN COMFORT**®

Ingredients should be room temperature. Grate cheese; cream together with butter. Add **SOUTHERN COMFORT**®; stir until smooth. Refrigerate in covered jar. *Makes about 2 cups*

Wright's

Smoky Cheese Spread

4 oz. Cheddar cheese, grated
1 8 oz. pkg. cream cheese
1 3 oz. wedge **ROQUEFORT Cheese** (optional)
1 tsp. **WRIGHT'S Hickory Liquid Smoke**™
Chopped parsley or chopped pecans

Bring cheeses to room temperature. Mix all ingredients, except parsley or pecans, in electric mixer or food processor. Shape into ball if desired, roll in parsley or pecans. Chill. Serve with assorted crackers.

Arnold Sorensin Spratt Spread

2 cans of **ARNOLD SORENSIN Spratts**
8 oz. of cream cheese, softened

Just drain the oil from the Spratts and blend the two ingredients together in a food processor or with a fork. Refrigerate for a few hours. Serve with melba toast, crackers or on bread of your choice.

Caraway Cheese Spread

2 cups (8 ounces) shredded Cheddar cheese
½ cup **MEADOW GOLD**® Cottage Cheese
¼ cup (½ stick) **MEADOW GOLD**® Butter, softened
1 teaspoon caraway seeds
1 teaspoon each: finely chopped onion, prepared mustard
½ teaspoon soy sauce
Chopped parsley

In mixing bowl, combine above ingredients except parsley. Beat until well blended. Chill mixture several hours. Shape into round ball; roll in chopped parsley.

Cheesy Corn Spread

12 oz. (3 cups) shredded sharp Cheddar cheese
½ cup dairy sour cream
½ cup salad dressing or mayonnaise
¼ cup finely chopped onion
½ teaspoon salt
12-oz. can **GREEN GIANT® MEXICORN® Golden
  Whole Kernel Corn with Sweet Peppers,** drained

Bring cheese to room temperature. In large bowl, crumble cheese
with fork or blend with mixer to form small bits. Mix in remaining
ingredients, except corn, until well blended. Stir in corn. Cover;
chill several hours or overnight. Can be stored in the refrigerator
up to 1 week. Serve with raw vegetables or crackers. *3½ cups*

High Altitude—Above 3500 Feet: No change.

NUTRITIONAL INFORMATION PER SERVING

SERVING SIZE:		PERCENT U.S. RDA	
1 Tablespoon		PER SERVING	
Calories	40	Protein	3
Protein	2 g	Vitamin A	2
Carbohydrate	2 g	Vitamin C	*
Fat	3 g	Thiamine	*
Sodium	95 mg	Riboflavin	2
Potassium	15 mg	Niacin	*
		Calcium	5
		Iron	*

*Contains less than 2% of the U.S. RDA of this nutrient.

Lindsay.

Lindsay® Ripe Olive "Fillers"

A quick and easy appetizer to spread on crackers or melba toast is
prepared by combining 1 (3 oz.) package of cream cheese, ¼ cup
LINDSAY® Chopped Ripe Olives, 1 (2¼ oz.) can deviled ham
and ½ to 1 teaspoon horseradish.

DANNON® YOGURT

Spinach and Yogurt Appetizer

1 pound spinach, washed, drained, stemmed and
  coarsely chopped
½ cup water
3 tablespoons olive oil
1 small onion, finely chopped
1 cup **DANNON® Plain Lowfat Yogurt**
1 small clove garlic, crushed, or to taste
½ teaspoon crushed dried mint
Salt and freshly ground black pepper to taste
2 tablespoons finely chopped toasted walnut meats

In a heavy saucepan combine the spinach with the water and bring
to a boil over high heat. Reduce the heat to low, cover, and
simmer 10 minutes. Drain and squeeze the spinach dry. In a heavy
skillet heat the oil over moderate flame. Add the onion and sauté a
few minutes. Remove from the heat.
  In a mixing bowl combine the yogurt, garlic, mint, and salt and
pepper until well blended. Gradually stir in the contents of the
skillet and mix   ly. Taste for seasoning. Transfer to a
serving bowl, cover, and chill. Serve sprinkled with the walnuts.
Serves 4

California Spread

1 can **KING OSCAR Sardines**
1 ripe California avocado
2 Tbsp. grated onion
2 Tbsp. lemon juice
½ cup sour cream
Dash **TABASCO®**
Salt
Parsley

Mash sardines and avocado. Add remaining ingredients, except
parsley. Blend thoroughly. Sprinkle with chopped fresh parsley.
Serve with crackers or toast fingers.

Hot Bacon Spread

1 package (8 oz.) **OSCAR MAYER Bacon**
2 packages (3 oz. each) cream cheese
2 tablespoons milk
2 tablespoons finely chopped onion
½ teaspoon horseradish

Preheat oven to 375°. Cook bacon until crisp; drain and crumble.
Blend cream cheese with milk. Stir in onion, horseradish and
crumbled bacon*. Spread in individual casserole or small oven-
proof platter. Bake 15 minutes. Serve with crackers or fresh
vegetable relishes. *Makes 1 cup*

*A few tablespoons of bacon may be reserved to sprinkle on top of
mixture before baking.

Smoky Salmon Spread

1 can **ALASKA Canned Salmon**
1 package (8 oz.) cream cheese, softened
1 tablespoon lemon juice
2 teaspoons *each* grated onion and prepared horseradish
¼ teaspoon liquid smoke
⅛ teaspoon salt
3 drops bottled hot pepper sauce
⅓ cup chopped pecans
Assorted crackers

Drain and flake salmon. Combine salmon, cream cheese, lemon
juice, onion, horseradish, liquid smoke, salt and hot pepper sauce.
Blend together thoroughly. Chill several hours. Shape salmon
mixture into a ball. Roll in nuts. Chill. Serve as a spread with crisp
crackers. *Makes about 2½ cups*

Favorite recipe from the **Alaska Seafood Marketing Institute**

KNOX®

Fishermen's Best Spread

2 envelopes **KNOX® Unflavored Gelatine**
½ cup cold water
1 cup boiling water
2 cups (16 oz.) sour cream
1 cup **WISH-BONE® Thousand Island Dressing**
2 cans (7 oz. ea.) tuna or salmon, drained and flaked*
¼ cup finely chopped onion
1 teaspoon dill weed

In large bowl, sprinkle unflavored gelatine over cold water; let stand 1 minute. Add boiling water and stir until gelatine is completely dissolved. With wire whip or rotary beater, blend in sour cream and Thousand Island dressing. Fold in remaining ingredients. Turn into 6-cup mold or bowl; chill until firm.

Makes about 5½ cups spread

*Substitution: Use canned shrimp or crabmeat.

Note: Recipe can be halved. Turn into 3-cup mold or bowl.

LAWRY'S®

Assorted Cheese Spreads

11 ounces cream cheese
2 tablespoons half and half

Cream together and season with one of the following combinations:

Herbed

¼ teaspoon EACH: **LAWRY'S® Pinch of Herbs**, **LAWRY'S® Seasoned Salt** and paprika

Garlic

1 teaspoon **LAWRY'S® Garlic Powder with Parsley**
½ teaspoon **LAWRY'S® Seasoned Salt**

Peppery

½ teaspoon EACH: **LAWRY'S® Seasoned Salt** and **LAWRY'S® Seasoned Pepper**

Blend together thoroughly. Chill several hours before transporting and serving. *Makes about 1½ cups*

Gingered Ham Spread

2 diced cooked **ATALANTA/KRAKUS/POLKA Polish Ham**
½ cup Mandarin oranges, cut-up
¼ cup chopped toasted almonds
¼ cup seedless grapes, cut-up
2 tablespoons minced green pepper
½ teaspoon garlic salt
⅛ teaspoon pepper
½ cup mayonnaise or salad dressing
Assorted breads

Combine all ingredients, except bread. Blend well and chill until ready to serve. Spread on breads. *Makes about 10 servings*

THE CHRISTIAN BROTHERS®
Cheery Cheese Spread

½ cup **THE CHRISTIAN BROTHERS® Ruby Port**
¼ cup cream
½ tsp. paprika
1 tsp. grated onion
¾ lb. sharp Cheddar cheese, diced
¼ lb. blue cheese, crumbled

Combine ingredients in blender; whirl until smooth. Pack into small crocks or containers to store in refrigerator or give as gifts. *2 cups*

Carl Buddig
Piccalitoes

1 package **BUDDIG Smoked Sliced Beef** or **Peppered Beef**, finely chopped
1 teaspoon minced onion
1 tablespoon butter
1 3-ounce package cream cheese
Saltines or crisp rye crackers

Cook **BUDDIG Beef** and onion in butter until beef is slightly crisp. Add to cream cheese and blend. Spread on crackers.

Dips

Heavenly Ham Dip in a Bread Bowl

2 (one-pound) loaves **BRIDGFORD Frozen Bread Dough**
1 Tablespoon salt mixed in 1 cup of ice water
1 8-ounce package cream cheese
1 cup sour cream
4 ounces **BRIDGFORD Thinly Sliced Ham**, finely chopped
2 Tablespoons chopped green pepper
¼ cup finely chopped green onion
½ Tablespoon Worcestershire Sauce

DAY BEFORE SERVING, MAKE BREAD BOWL:
Let one loaf frozen dough thaw to room temperature. Form thawed dough into large round ball and place in lightly greased 9″ pie plate. (Or, if making individual muffins, divide dough into 12 pieces and place in lightly greased muffin pan.) Let dough rise 1½ hours at room temperature, basting dough every 30 minutes with salt and ice water mixture. When dough has increased to 3 times its original size, place in preheated 350° oven and bake 25-30 minutes. Remove baked loaf from pie plate immediately and let cool completely. When cool, cut circle around top of loaf one inch in from edge. Remove top and save. Hollow out center of loaf to form bowl for dip. Place hollowed loaf, top off, back in oven for 5-8 minutes at 375°. Cool. Let stand uncovered at room temperature overnight.

Take second loaf frozen dough from freezer and place in refrigerator overnight. This will be used to make pieces for dipping.

NEXT DAY, MAKE DIP:
Simply mix cream cheese and sour cream together until smooth. Add all remaining ingredients and pour into center of bread bowl. Serve with Mini Bread Balls*, or a garnish of fresh vegetables for dipping.

To serve warm, replace bread-lid on bowl, wrap in foil and bake at 300° for 1-1½ hours.

*TO MAKE MINI BREAD BALLS FOR DIPPING:
Remove second loaf of dough from refrigerator. Divide thawed dough into 36 small pieces. Place on lightly greased cookie sheet. Let dough rest for 30 minutes at room temperature, then bake in preheated 350° oven for 20 minutes. Place pieces around large dip-filled bread bowl and use for dipping.

TABASCO®
Tabasco® Dip Piquante

1 package (8 ounces) cream cheese
½ teaspoon **TABASCO®**
3 tablespoons mayonnaise
1 tablespoon horseradish
1 teaspoon minced onion
¼ teaspoon celery salt

Soften cream cheese in mixing bowl. Add **TABASCO®** and mayonnaise and beat until smooth. Stir in remaining ingredients. Use as dip for potato chips, pretzel sticks, Melba toast or crackers.

Makes about 1¼ cups

Note: The flavor improves on standing. Keep in refrigerator several hours before serving.

Ham Sticks With Yogurt Dill Dip
(Low Calorie)

Cut contents of one 8 ounce package of **OSCAR MAYER 95% Fat-Free Ham Steaks** into julienne strips. For dip, mix 1 (16 oz.) container plain yogurt with ½ tsp. dill weed and 2 tsp. dehydrated minced onion. Chill.

Makes 8 servings

Calories: One serving (¼ cup dip; ½ ham steak) contains 50 calories.

Old El Paso® Guacamole

2 large ripe avocados, peeled, pitted and sliced
1 jar (8 oz.) **OLD EL PASO®** Taco Sauce
½ cup chopped onion
2 tablespoons lemon or lime juice
1 teaspoon salt
½ teaspoon garlic powder
1 box (7½ oz.) **OLD EL PASO® NACHIPS** Tortilla Chips

Blend avocado slices, taco sauce, onion, juice, salt and garlic powder in blender or food processor. Chill. Serve with **NACHIPS**.

Guacamole

Mash 2 **CALAVO®** Avocados. Blend in a chopped tomato, ¼ cup grated onion, ½ teaspoon seasoned salt, 1 tablespoon fresh **CALAVO®** Lime Juice. Spread generously on hamburgers. Or serve as dip with corn chips. (For convenience, try **CALAVO® Frozen Fresh Guacamole** in flavors.)

Makes 2½ cups

Dieters' Guacamole With Corn Chips
(Low Calorie/Low Cholesterol)

1 pound asparagus (2 cups)
1 tablespoon fresh lemon juice
1½ tablespoons finely chopped onion
1 medium tomato, chopped
1 teaspoon salt
½ teaspoon **SWEETLITE™ Liquid Fructose**
¼ teaspoon ground cumin
¼ teaspoon chili powder
⅛ teaspoon garlic powder
Dash **TABASCO®** Sauce
½ cup sour cream
1 scant tablespoon (1 envelope) unflavored gelatin
¼ cup water
Fat-Free Corn Chips*

1. Wash the asparagus and break off the tough ends. Cut the spears into 1-inch pieces and cook in a steamer until just fork tender, about 4 minutes.
2. Cool the cooked asparagus to room temperature.
3. Put the cooled asparagus and all other ingredients except the gelatin, water and corn chips into a blender container and blend until smooth.
4. Put the gelatin in a small saucepan and add the water. Allow to soften for 5 minutes.
5. Place the pan on low heat, stirring constantly, until the gelatin is completely dissolved. **Do not allow it to come to a boil.**
6. Add the dissolved gelatin to the blender container and blend on low speed until thoroughly mixed.
7. Pour the guacamole in a bowl and refrigerate until firm.
8. Serve with Fat-Free Corn Chips, as a dip, sauce or even as a salad dressing. NO AVOCADO!!! FEWER CALORIES!!!

Makes 2 cups

¼ cup contains approximately:
   ½ vegetable exchange
   ½ fat exchange
   36 calories
   8 mg. cholesterol

*Fat-Free Corn Chips

6 corn tortillas
Salt

1. Cut each tortilla into six pie-shaped pieces.
2. Spread the tortilla sections on a cookie sheet and lightly salt them.
3. Bake in a preheated 400° oven for 10 minutes.
4. Remove from the oven and turn each corn chip over and return them to the oven for 3-5 minutes or until crisp.

Fat-Free Corn Chips are fresher tasting and lower in calories than commercially prepared corn chips. If you prefer smaller chips, cross-cut the tortillas in strips instead of triangles. You may also wish to sprinkle the tortillas with seasoned salt, cumin or chili powder for flavored Fat-Free Corn Chips.

Makes 36 corn chips

Each 6 chips contain approximately:
   1 bread exchange
   70 calories
   0 mg. cholesterol

Avocado Cream Cheese Dunk

Select a firm but not ripe avocado and split it lengthwise, removing the seed. Scoop out the meat, mash and mix with the following ingredients: 2-3 oz. packages cream cheese softened with 2 Tbsp. **DuBONNET Blanc** aperitif wine, ½ tsp. grated onion, 1 Tbsp. lemon juice, 1 tsp. salt. Return the dunk to the avocado shell and serve well chilled.

Coral Cream Dip

Combine thoroughly 1 package (8 ounces) softened cream cheese, ½ cup **HEINZ Tomato Ketchup**, 1 tablespoon prepared mustard, 1½ teaspoons grated onion, ½ teaspoon salt. Cover; chill to blend flavors. Serve dip with your favorite chips and chilled fresh vegetables. *Makes about 1⅔ cups*

PET.
Vegetable Dip
(Low Calorie/Low Cholesterol)

1 can (8 oz.) **PET® Imitation Sour Cream**
2 teaspoons instant minced onion
½ teaspoon garlic salt
¼ cup minced radishes
¼ cup minced green pepper
3 drops hot sauce

Combine all ingredients. Chill to blend the flavors. Serve with crackers, chips, or fresh crisp vegetables.

Makes about 1¼ cups dip

Blue Cheese Dip or Dressing

1 pkg. (8 oz.) cream cheese, softened
½ teaspoon garlic salt (or as desired)
2 tablespoons lemon juice
½ cup **MILNOT®**
½ cup (approx. 4 oz.) crumbled blue cheese

Beat cream cheese until fluffy, add garlic salt and lemon juice gradually, then add **MILNOT®**. Blend well. Fold in crumbled blue cheese. Serve as a dip or on vegetable salads.

Yield: approx. 2 cups

Zesty Cheese Dip

Combine thoroughly 1 package (8 ounces) softened cream cheese, ⅓ cup crumbled blue cheese, ⅓ cup **HEINZ Tomato Ketchup**, 1 teaspoon prepared horseradish, and ¼ teaspoon salt. Cover; chill to blend flavors. Serve dips with your favorite chips and chilled fresh vegetables. *Makes about 1⅔ cups*

Best Foods
HELLMANN'S.
Yogurt Lime Dip
(Low Cholesterol)

1 cup plain low-fat yogurt
½ cup **BEST FOODS®/HELLMAN'S® Real Mayonnaise**
1½ teaspoons grated lime rind
1 teaspoon lime juice

Stir together all ingredients. Cover; chill. Serve with strawberries, melon balls, apple and banana slices. Or, cauliflowerettes, carrot or celery sticks. *Makes 1½ cups*

Cholesterol: 5 mg per 2 tablespoon serving

Eggplant Dip

1 medium eggplant, cubed
1 medium green pepper, chopped
1 large tomato, chopped
1 medium purple onion, chopped
1 large clove garlic, minced
2 tablespoons butter or olive oil
1 cup chili sauce
⅓ cup water

In large skillet, cook vegetables in butter until tender. Add sauce and water. Simmer uncovered 5 minutes. Serve warm or chilled with **PEPPERIDGE FARM® Lightly Salted** or **Cheese Goldfish Thins**. *Makes about 3 cups*

Mexicali Dip

1 lb. **VELVEETA Pasteurized Process Cheese Spread**, cubed
1 16-oz. can tomatoes, drained, chopped
1 4-oz. can green chilies, drained, chopped
1 tablespoon instant minced onion
Corn or tortilla chips

Combine process cheese spread, tomatoes, chilies and onion in saucepan; cook over low heat until process cheese spread melts. Serve hot with corn chips. *3 cups*

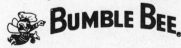

Horseradish Dip

1 can (15½ oz.) **BUMBLE BEE® Pink Salmon**
1 package (8 oz.) cream cheese, softened
¼ cup dairy sour cream
¼ cup prepared horseradish
½ teaspoon salt
⅛ teaspoon garlic powder
Crisp romaine lettuce
Paprika
Crackers
Celery sticks

(Continued)

(Continued)

Drain salmon. Remove skin, if desired. Mash bones. Beat cream cheese, sour cream, horseradish, salt and garlic powder until smooth. Beat in salmon and bones until blended. Arrange romaine lettuce in a bowl. Spoon in salmon mixture. Sprinkle with paprika. Serve with crackers and celery sticks.   *Makes 6 to 8 servings*

Green Goddess Dip for Jays Potato Chips

1 clove garlic, grated
2 tablespoons anchovy paste
3 tablespoons finely chopped chives
1 tablespoon lemon juice
1 tablespoon tarragon wine vinegar
½ cup heavy sour cream
1 cup mayonnaise
⅓ cup finely chopped parsley
Coarse salt
Coarsely ground black pepper

Combine ingredients in order given. Pour in serving bowl and chill. Canned whole anchovies may be chopped fine and substituted for the anchovy paste. Coarse salt may be purchased in pound containers. Lacking a pepper grinder use a pestle to mash the peppercorns in a mortar. Serve with **JAYS Potato Chips**.

Slender Sliced Beef Party Dip

2 packages **ECKRICH® Slender Sliced Beef**, chopped
1 cup commercial sour cream
1 3-ounce package cream cheese
2 tsp. horseradish

Combine sour cream, softened cream cheese, and horseradish. Fold in chopped Slender Sliced Beef. Serve with chips or crisp crackers.   *Makes about 2½ cups*

Holiday—Sausage Stroganoff Dip

1 clove garlic
2 lbs. **JIMMY DEAN® Sausage**
4 Tbsp. flour
2 cups beef broth
2 onions chopped (medium)
1 cup mushrooms sliced (canned or fresh)
½ stick butter
2 tsp. soy sauce
2 Tbsp. Worcestershire
1 tsp. dry mustard
Salt-pepper-paprika
TABASCO® to taste
2 cups sour cream
Party rye or pumpernickel bread toasted

Rub large skillet with garlic; heat and brown sausage. Crumble sausage with a fork. Sprinkle sausage with flour; add beef broth. Simmer until slightly thickened & set aside. Sauté onions and mushrooms in butter until onions are tender. Add onions, mushrooms and seasonings to sausage mixture. Cook until mixture bubbles—remove from heat and add sour cream. Keep hot in chafing dish. Serve with toasted party rye or party size pumpernickel.

(To double recipe, use only 3 onions. Freezes well before adding sour cream.) If you have leftovers, pour over rice.
Makes approximately 1½ qts.

Gallo® Salame Party Dip

6 ounces **GALLO® Italian Dry Salame**
12 ounces sour cream

Finely chop **GALLO® Italian Dry Salame**. Measure by weight both chopped **GALLO® Salame** and sour cream before mixing to insure 1 part **GALLO® Salame** to 2 parts sour cream. Mix well. Refrigerate minimum of 2 hours for firmness. Serve on celery, crackers, sliced cucumbers, cauliflower, cherry tomatoes, or chips.

Butter Buds® Cottage Cheese Dip
(Low Calorie/Low Fat)

1 cup low-fat cottage cheese
1 packet **BUTTER BUDS®**
1 tablespoon Worcestershire sauce
4 teaspoons minced onion
1 teaspoon horseradish
1 teaspoon caraway seeds
Freshly ground pepper to taste
Dash paprika (optional)

Place cheese in blender container. Cover and process at medium speed 30 seconds, or until smooth. Add **BUTTER BUDS®**, Worcestershire, onion, and horseradish; process 10 seconds, or until well mixed. Scrape into bowl and stir in caraway and pepper. Garnish with paprika. Serve with Dippers*.   *1 cup*

Per Serving (2 tablespoons): Calories: 35; Fat: trace. By using **BUTTER BUDS®** instead of butter in this recipe you have saved 180 calories and 70 mg cholesterol per serving.

*Dippers
(Low Calorie/Low Fat/Low Sodium)

1 pound lean flank steak
Freshly ground pepper to taste
1 pound fresh mushrooms
1 pound fresh string beans
1 pound fresh broccoli
1 medium head (about 1¼ pounds) cauliflower

Preheat broiler. Sprinkle steak with pepper. Cut into thin strips and arrange on rack of broiler pan. Broil about 5 minutes, or until done as desired. Wash vegetables well and trim leaves and ends. Slice mushrooms and beans. Cut broccoli and cauliflower into bite-size pieces. Arrange meat and vegetables on serving platter surrounding bowl of Cottage Cheese Dip.   *12 servings*

Per Serving (Dippers only): Calories: 90; Fat 2 g; Sodium 20 mg

Twin Cheese Dip

About ¾ pound (12 oz.) sharp Cheddar cheese
1 package (4 oz.) **ROQUEFORT Cheese**
1 clove garlic
¾ cup **COCA-COLA®**
2 tablespoons soft margarine
1 tablespoon grated onion
1½ teaspoons Worcestershire sauce
1 teaspoon dry mustard
¼ teaspoon salt
⅛ teaspoon **TABASCO®**

Grate Cheddar cheese into large mixing bowl. Add crumbled **ROQUEFORT**. Put garlic through a press; add to cheeses with ½ cup of the **COCA-COLA®** and remaining ingredients. Beat with electric mixer on low speed until blended. Gradually add remaining **COCA-COLA®** then beat on high speed until mixture is fairly smooth, light and fluffy. Pack into covered container. Chill. Best if refrigerated overnight. A piquant, fluffy cheese dip for raw vegetables, a spread for cocktail breads or crackers, or even a sandwich filling. This keeps very well for a week or more.

Makes about 3 cups

Best Foods.
HELLMANN'S.
Spinach Dip

2 cups **BEST FOODS®/HELLMAN'S® Real Mayonnaise**
½ cup parsley sprigs
½ small onion, cut up
1 small clove garlic
1 tablespoon lemon juice
¼ teaspoon pepper
1 package (10 oz.) frozen chopped spinach, thawed, well drained on paper towels

In blender container place **Real Mayonnaise**, parsley, onion, garlic, lemon juice, pepper and spinach; cover. Blend at high speed 10 to 20 seconds or until vegetables are finely chopped. Cover; refrigerate at least 4 hours or overnight to blend flavors. If desired, serve with chips. *Makes 2¾ cups*

FOOD PROCESSOR METHOD:
In bowl of food processor with metal blade place **Real Mayonnaise**, parsley, onion, garlic, lemon juice, pepper and spinach; cover. With on and off motion process until pureed. Continue as above.

Note: Dip may be prepared up to 2 days ahead.

Sweet-Sour Dip

Mix ⅓ cup pineapple, apricot or peach preserves, ⅓ cup tomato catsup and 1 Tbsp. vinegar. Add soy sauce to taste and contents of mustard packet. Serve with **JENO'S® Egg Rolls**.

Lipton.

Lipton® California Dip

In small bowl, blend 1 envelope **LIPTON® Onion Soup Mix** with 2 cups (16 oz.) sour cream; chill.

Makes about 2 cups

VARIATIONS:

California Ginger Dip

Add 1 teaspoon ground ginger.

California Vegetable Dip

Add 1 cup each finely chopped green pepper and tomato and 2 teaspoons chili powder.

California Blue Cheese Dip

Add ¼ pound crumbled blue cheese and ¼ cup finely chopped walnuts.

California Seafood Dip

Add 1 cup finely chopped cooked shrimp, clams or crab meat, ¼ cup chili sauce and 1 tablespoon horseradish.

Skinny Dip

Substitute 2 cups (16 oz.) plain yogurt for sour cream.

Breakstone's
Since 1882

Cottage Cheese Dip

1 cup **BREAKSTONE'S® Smooth and Creamy Style Cottage Cheese**
¼ cup **KRAFT Creamy Cucumber Dressing**
2 crisply cooked bacon slices, crumbled
1 tablespoon green onion slices

Combine all ingredients; mix well. Chill. Serve with vegetable dippers. *1¼ cups*

Mystery
Hors d'Oeuvre-Relish

Snip 1 cup pitted dates into sixths. In a saucepan, combine with ½ cup chili sauce, 1 teaspoon grated orange rind, ½ cup orange juice, 2 tablespoons chopped onion, 1 teaspoon minced, seeded canned green chiles **or** 1 or more teaspoons green salsa sauce, 1 oz. unsweetened chocolate, grated; bring to rolling boil, stirring often; remove from heat; stir in ¼ cup coarsely chopped **BLUE RIBBON® Natural Almonds**, roasted. Chill. Serve with corn chips.

Makes 1¾ cups

Mild Pepper Dip

1¾ cups (16 oz.) **KAUKAUNA®** Cheese Mild Pepper
  Buttery Spread™
1 can (4 oz.) chopped green chilies, drained
¼ cup chopped ripe olives
¼ cup chopped green onions
¼ cup dairy sour cream
Bread sticks or tortilla chips

Heat cheese in medium saucepan over low heat until melted.
Blend in remaining ingredients except bread sticks or chips. Serve
hot with bread sticks or chips.   *Makes 3 cups*

Original Ranch Dip

1 pint sour cream
1 packet **HIDDEN VALLEY ORIGINAL RANCH®**
  Salad Dressing

Combine sour cream and Salad Dressing mix; stir to blend. Chill.
For variety add any one of the following ingredients in amounts to
satisfy taste: dill weed, well-drained minced clams, shrimp or
crab.   *Makes 2 cups dip*

Roquefort Sour Cream Dip

Combine 1 cup dairy sour cream, ¼ cup crumbled
ROQUEFORT, 1 scant tablespoon prepared mustard and 1 tablespoon capers; mix well.   *Makes over 1 cup of basic dip*

Favorite recipe from the **Roquefort Association, Inc.**

Angostura® Vegetable Dip

1 pint sour cream
1 package (2.3 oz.) Russian salad dressing mix
2 teaspoons **ANGOSTURA®** Aromatic Bitters

Mix all ingredients together and blend well.   *Yield: 2 cups*

Hot Artichoke 'n Herbs Dip

⅓ cup **WISH-BONE®** Sour Cream & Italian Herbs
  Dressing
1 package (9 oz.) frozen artichoke hearts, thawed and
  coarsely chopped
¼ cup grated Parmesan cheese
Buttered bread crumbs
Suggested dippers—raw carrot or celery sticks, whole
  mushrooms or sliced zucchini

Preheat oven to 350. In blender or food processor, combine **Sour
Cream and Italian Herbs Dressing**, artichokes and cheese;
process at high speed until blended. Turn into 2-cup casserole, top
with bread crumbs. Bake 30 minutes or until heated through.
Serve with Suggested Dippers.   *Makes about 2 cups dip*

Hot Sausage-Bean Dip

½ pound **TENNESSEE PRIDE®** Country Sausage
1 16-ounce can pork and beans in tomato sauce
2 ounces sharp process American cheese, shredded (½
  cup)
2 tablespoons catsup
½ teaspoon prepared mustard
Few drops bottled hot pepper sauce

Cook **TENNESSEE PRIDE®** Country Sausage in skillet until
it loses its pink color; stir to break up sausage and drain off fat. In
blender combine sausage with beans, shredded cheese, catsup,
mustard and hot pepper sauce; blend till smooth, stopping occasionally to scrape down sides. Return to skillet. Heat. Serve with
corn chips or assorted crackers.   *Makes 2½ cups*

Hot Bean and Cheese Dip

1 11½-ounce can condensed bean with bacon soup
1 cup (4 ounces) shredded sharp American cheese
¼ cup chopped green chilies
1 teaspoon instant minced onion
Dash garlic powder
¼ cup water
LA FIESTAᵀ·ᴹ· **Tortilla Strips**

In saucepan, combine soup, cheese, chilies, onion, garlic powder,
and water. Heat slowly, stirring constantly, till heated through.
Transfer to fondue pot or small chafing dish. Keep warm over
fondue or chafing dish burner. Add water to thin, as necessary.
Serve with tortilla strips for dippers.

          Makes about 2 cups dip

Quick Draw Dip

1 - 15 oz. can **WOLF®** Brand Plain Chili
1 cup (8 oz.) jar picante sauce
2 - 11 oz. cans condensed Cheddar cheese soup
  (undiluted) OR
2 lb. pasteurized process cheese spread (cubed and
  melted)

Combine **WOLF®** Brand Chili, picante sauce, and Cheddar
cheese soup (undiluted) *OR* melted process cheese in sauce pan.
Warm thoroughly over low heat stirring frequently. Serve warm
with tortilla chips.

Hot Bean Dip

1 can (16 ounces) **VAN CAMP'S®** Pork and Beans
2 Tablespoons minced pickled jalapeño pepper
4 ounces pasteurized process cheese spread, cubed
Corn chips

In blender purée pork and beans and jalapeño pepper. Pour into saucepan, add cheese and heat until cheese is melted. Garnish with additional chopped jalapeño pepper if desired. Serve with corn chips. *About 2 cups*

MICROWAVE METHOD:
In blender purée pork and beans and jalapeño pepper. Pour into bowl, add cheese, cover, and microcook 2 to 3 minutes, or until cheese is melted. Stir twice. Serve with corn chips.

Bean Dip

- 1-16 oz. can **GEBHARDT®'S Refried Beans**
- ¼ cup chopped onions
- 1 clove garlic, minced
- 1 tablespoon oil
- ¼ teaspoon salt
- 1 teaspoon **GEBHARDT®'S Chili Powder**
- 1 tablespoon **GEBHARDT®'S Picante Sauce***
- ¼ cup water

Heat oil in a skillet and brown onions and garlic. Add refried beans and stir until hot. Stir in salt, picante sauce, chili powder, and water. Simmer about 5 minutes.

*Picante Sauce

If **GEBHARDT®'S Picante Sauce** is not available, use this recipe.

- 1-10 oz. can tomatoes & green chilies
- 1 jalapeño pepper, chopped
- ½ cup chopped onion
- ¼ teaspoon garlic salt

Pour can of tomatoes and green chilies in a blender or food processor. Add 1 medium chopped jalapeño, without seeds. Add ½ cup chopped onion and ¼ teaspoon garlic salt. Turn on to "blend" for about 10 seconds.

Serve as a dip by itself or use as hot sauce in cooking other dishes or as a hot sauce over your favorite Mexican food recipes at the table. Keep your leftover in a jar and refrigerate.

Note: Add half the jalapeño to start with, adding more later to taste.

Red Boy Bean Dip

- 1 can (1 lb.) refried beans
- 2 cups (1 pt.) **DARIGOLD Sour Cream**
- 2 cups (8 oz.) **DARIGOLD Red Boy Cheese**, shredded
- 1 chili pepper, chopped
- 1 tsp. chili powder
- 1 tsp. cumin
- ½ tsp. oregano
- ½ tsp. garlic powder

In a saucepan combine refried beans with **DARIGOLD Sour Cream** and **DARIGOLD Red Boy Cheese**. Cook over medium heat until warm and cheese is melted. Stir in chili and seasonings. Serve either warm or cold. Use vegies or tortilla chips as dippers. *Makes 3 cups*

Fiesta Bean Dip

- 1 can (8¼ ounces) **ROSARITA® Refried Beans**
- 2 tablespoons finely chopped onion
- 3 tablespoons dairy sour cream
- 2 tablespoons **ROSARITA® Taco Sauce**
- 2 tablespoons tomato paste
- ½ teaspoon chili powder
- ¼ teaspoon salt
- ⅛ teaspoon **ROSARITA® Hot Sauce**

Combine above ingredients, mixing well. Chill, covered, for several hours. Serve with tortilla chips. *1⅓ cups*

Fiesta Dip

- 1 can (16 oz.) refried beans
- 1 can (4 oz.) diced green chiles
- ½ cup prepared **HIDDEN VALLEY ORIGINAL RANCH® Salad Dressing**
- 2 teaspoons taco sauce

In a bowl, blend together above ingredients; chill. Suggested dippers: Tortilla chips and avocado slices. *Makes 2 cups dip*

Caviar Yogurt Dip

- ⅔ cup plain yogurt
- 2 oz. **ROMANOFF® Caviar***
- 1 Tbsp. minced parsley
- 2 tsp. grated onion and juice
- 1 tsp. prepared mustard

Combine all ingredients. Serve at once or cover and chill. Just before serving, stir. Good with unsalted crackers or crisp raw vegetables. *Makes about 1 cup dip, enough for 6 to 8*

***ROMANOFF® Red Lumpfish** or **Salmon Caviar** suggested.

Campbell's

Hot Onion Dip

- 1 can (10½ ounces) **CAMPBELL'S Condensed Cream of Onion Soup**
- 1 package (8 ounces) cream cheese, softened
- 2 tablespoons chili sauce
- 1 tablespoon chopped hot cherry peppers

With electric mixer or rotary beater, gradually blend soup into cream cheese. Beat just until smooth (overbeating makes dip thin). Stir in chili sauce and peppers; chill. Serve with crackers or chips. *Makes about 2 cups*

Seasoned Fish Dip

2 cups cooked, flaked fish*
1 cup large curd cottage cheese
¾ cup sour cream
2 tablespoons chicken seasoned stock base
1 tablespoon chopped pimiento, drained
1 tablespoon chopped parsley
Chopped parsley (garnish)
Assorted chips, crackers or raw vegetables

*Drop fish fillets into boiling salted water and cook just until flesh is opaque and flakes easily when tested with a fork. Remove any skin and bones.

Combine all ingredients except garnish and crackers. Chill one hour. Garnish with chopped parsley. Serve with chips, crackers or vegetables. *Makes approximately 3 cups of dip*

Favorite recipe from the **Florida Department of Natural Resources**

Spicy Seafood Dip

1 cup (8 oz.) **BREYERS® Plain Yogurt**
¼ cup mayonnaise
1¼ teaspoons curry powder
1 tablespoon finely chopped onion
2 teaspoons lemon juice
½ teaspoon salt
Dash of pepper
1 can (6½ oz.) crab, tuna fish, or shrimp; drained, flaked, or chopped

Combine all ingredients; mix well. Chill several hours. Serve with raw vegetables or crackers. *Makes 1½ cups*

Curried Tuna Dipping Sauce

2 cans (6½ or 7 ounces each) tuna, drained
1 cup cored, chopped apple, (do not pare)
1 cup plain yogurt
1 cup cottage cheese
¼ cup chopped almonds
¼ cup chopped chutney
¼ cup chopped onion
2 tablespoons raisins
1 tablespoon curry powder
1 teaspoon salt

In a medium bowl, flake tuna. Mix in remaining ingredients. Chill 1 hour. Serve with Melba toast, breadsticks, crackers and/or carrot/celery sticks. *Yield: About 4½ cups*

Favorite recipe from the **Tuna Research Foundation**

Spectacular Shrimp Spread

½ pound cooked, peeled and deveined rock shrimp
1 can (13 ounces) artichoke hearts, drained
1 cup mayonnaise*
½ cup Parmesan cheese
¼ teaspoon lemon pepper
⅛ teaspoon salt
Dash cayenne pepper
Melba Toast or assorted crackers

Finely chop rock shrimp and artichoke hearts. Add mayonnaise, cheese and seasonings; mix well. Place mixture in a 9-inch pie plate or 1-quart shallow baking dish. Bake at 400°F., for 10 minutes or until hot and bubbly. Serve hot with Melba Toast or crackers.

*½ cup mayonnaise and ½ cup plain yogurt may be substituted for 1 cup mayonnaise.

Favorite recipe from the **Gulf and South Atlantic Fisheries Development Foundation, Inc.**

Gerber®
Dilly Shrimp Dip

1 can (4½ oz.) shrimp, rinsed and drained
1 tablespoon lemon juice
1 package (3 oz.) cream cheese, softened
2 tablespoons milk
1 jar (4½ oz.) **GERBER® Strained Carrots**
¼ cup salad dressing
2 tablespoons finely chopped green onion
½ teaspoon dill weed
½ teaspoon **TABASCO® Sauce**
Salt and pepper to taste

Combine shrimp and lemon juice in small bowl. Toss well. Drain. Chop shrimp finely and set aside.

Beat cream cheese in medium bowl. Gradually add milk, carrots, and salad dressing, blending until smooth. Add onions, dill weed, **TABASCO® Sauce**, salt, and pepper. Stir in chopped shrimp. Cover and refrigerate until ready to serve.

Yield: Approximately 1⅔ cups

Your Own Shrimp Dip

1 can (4½ ounces) **LOUISIANA BRAND Shrimp**
2 teaspoons instant onion flakes
1 chicken bouillon cube
2 packages (3 ounces each) cream cheese
½ teaspoon Worcestershire sauce
¼ teaspoon hot pepper sauce
1 tablespoon lemon juice
2 tablespoons minced fresh parsley

Drain shrimp and chop coarsely. Soften onion flakes and dissolve bouillon cube in ⅓ cup hot water. Combine with cheese and work to a smooth dip consistency. Add all other seasonings and shrimp. *Makes 1¾ cups*

Holiday Crab Dip

1 (6-oz.) package **WAKEFIELD® Crabmeat**
1 (8-oz.) package softened cream cheese
⅓ cup mayonnaise
1 teaspoon prepared mustard with horseradish
1½ tablespoons dried onion
½ teaspoon seasoned salt
1 tablespoon coarsely chopped parsley
Dash of garlic powder

Thaw crabmeat, drain and separate into small chunks. Blend well cream cheese, mayonnaise, mustard, onion and seasoned salt. Fold in parsley, garlic powder and crabmeat. Serve hot or cold with crisp relishes or crackers.   *Makes 1¾ cups*

Crab Meat Dip

1 can **HIGH SEA Crab Meat**
2 Tbsp. mayonnaise
Dash of **TABASCO®**

Combine all ingredients in mixing bowl; serve over **RITZ Crackers**.

Mrs. Paul's

Lamaze Sauce

1 package **MRS. PAUL'S® Create A Sauce™**
1 cup mayonnaise
2 tablespoons chili sauce or ketchup
1 hard cooked egg, finely chopped
2 tablespoons celery, finely diced
2 tablespoons green pepper, finely diced
½ teaspoon Worcestershire sauce
Salt and pepper to taste

Combine all ingredients and mix thoroughly. Serve with **MRS. PAUL'S® French Fried Shrimp, French Fried Scallops** and **Deviled Crab Miniatures**.

Sealtest®

Creamy Clam Cheese Dip

1 cup **SEALTEST® Cottage Cheese**
2 tablespoons minced, drained canned clams
1 teaspoon finely snipped chives
Dash liquid hot-pepper sauce

Blend all ingredients well. Refrigerate in container with cover.
1 cup

REALEMON®

Manhattan Clam Dip

1 (8-ounce) container **BORDEN® Sour Cream**
¼ cup chili sauce or catsup
1 (6½-ounce) can **SNOW'S® Minced** *or* **Chopped Clams**, drained
¼ cup mayonnaise or salad dressing
1 tablespoon finely chopped green onion
1 teaspoon **REALEMON® Lemon Juice from Concentrate**
WISE® Potato Chips

In small bowl, combine all ingredients except chips; mix well. Chill before serving. Serve with chips. Refrigerate leftovers.
Makes about 1⅔ cups

Antipasto Verde

2 **CAPE GRANNY SMITH Apples**, unpared, cored, sliced into wedges
1 zucchini, unpared, cut into 3-inch strips
1 cucumber, sliced
2 cups raw broccoli flowerets
1 large green pepper, seeded cut into strips
1 small bunch scallions, cut into 3-inch lengths
3 ribs celery, cut into 3-inch sticks
Fresh parsley sprigs

Arrange apple wedges and vegetables on large serving platter. Garnish with fresh parsley. Serve chilled, with any of the following dips.*   *Yield: 6 to 8 appetizer servings*

*Savory Apple Cheese Dip

1 package (8 ounces) cream cheese, softened at room temperature
½ cup sour cream
3 tablespoons minced scallions
2 tablespoons minced parsley
2 tablespoons lime juice
1 teaspoon salt
1 **CAPE GRANNY SMITH Apple**, pared and shredded

Beat cream cheese until fluffy; beat in sour cream, scallions, parsley, lime juice and salt. Fold in shredded apple. Cover. Chill 1 hour before serving.   *Yield: About 1½ cups dip*

*Apple Curry Dip

1 cup cottage cheese
¼ cup mayonnaise
½ teaspoon curry powder
1 **CAPE GRANNY SMITH Apple**, pared and shredded

Beat cottage cheese until smooth; blend in mayonnaise and curry powder. Fold in shredded apple. Cover. Chill 1 hour before serving.   *Yield: About 1¼ cups dip*

*Apple Yogurt Dip

½ cup plain yogurt
2 tablespoons sugar
1 tablespoon lemon juice
2 teaspoons chopped fresh mint or 1 teaspoon dried mint leaves
1 **CAPE GRANNY SMITH Apple**, pared and shredded

Combine yogurt, sugar, lemon juice and mint; blend well. Fold in shredded apple. Cover. Chill 1 hour before serving.
Yield: About 1½ cups dip

*Dilly Apple Dip

1½ cups cottage cheese
1 tablespoon lemon juice
1 teaspoon minced onion
1 teaspoon salt
1 teaspoon dill
1 **CAPE GRANNY SMITH Apple**, pared and shredded

Beat cottage cheese until smooth. Stir in lemon juice, onion, salt, dill and shredded apple. Cover. Chill 1 hour before serving.
Yield: About 1½ cups dip

Dieters Strawberry Dip

1 cup ripe strawberries, halved
⅓ cup **DOMINO® Confectioners 10-X Powdered Sugar**
1 cup low fat cottage cheese

Place all ingredients in blender and blend until smooth, or beat with electric mixer until smooth. Use as Basic Fruit Dip.

Makes 1⅔ cups

Note: All dips, toppings and sauces should be refrigerated if not used immediately after preparation.

Party Snacks

Super Snacks

On a Toasted BAYS® English Muffin Half:

- spread with butter; sprinkle generously with Parmesan cheese; add garlic powder to taste; broil until cheese is bubbling.
- spread generously with softened cream cheese and top with strawberry jam.
- spread with softened cream cheese; top with slice of smoked salmon; sprinkle with lemon juice, chopped onion and capers (optional).
- spread with chunky style peanut butter; top with crumbled bacon.
- top with slice of Cheddar or American cheese; add one tablespoon chutney; broil until cheese melts.
- top with 3 tablespoons refried beans, then shredded, spiced "taco cheese"; broil until cheese is bubbling. For more spice, sprinkle chili powder on mixture before broiling.

Continental Sausage Sampler

HILLSHIRE FARM® Smoked Sausage (any variety)
Grated Swiss cheese
Sauerkraut or pizza sauce
Bacon slices

Cut sausage into 4″ pieces. Split lengthwise, ¾ through. Fill each with mixture of 2 Tbsp. grated Swiss cheese and 1 Tbsp. of either sauerkraut or pizza sauce. Wrap with bacon slice. Secure with a toothpick. Grill or broil (4″ from the heat) until bacon is done, turning often.

MICROWAVE METHOD:
Place bacon on paper towels and microwave 30 sec. per slice. Assemble as above. Place on microwave safe roasting rack or paper towels. Microwave, 1 lb. sausage, covered with paper towel, HIGH, 3-5 minutes or until bacon is crisp and sausage is hot, turning over once.

(Continued)

HILLSHIRE FARM® Sausage (any variety)
Sautéed green peppers and onions
Prepared stuffing mix
Grated Cheddar cheese
Seasoned mashed potatoes

Heat 4″ lengths of sausage 8 minutes at low simmer or split lengthwise to grill, broil or pan fry. Stuff with one of the suggested ingredients.

MICROWAVE METHOD:
Microwave sausage, in a covered dish, HIGH, 3 minutes per pound. Assemble as above.

Sausage Smorgasbord of Snacks

Party rye bread slices
Prepared mustard
HILLSHIRE FARM® Polska Kielbasa or Smoked Sausage (¼″ slices)
Sauerkraut, rinsed and drained
Swiss cheese slices, cut to fit bread
Dill pickle slices (chips)
Toothpicks

Spread each slice of party rye with mustard. Top with 2 slices sausage, 1 teaspoon sauerkraut, 1 slice Swiss cheese and 1 dill pickle slice. Secure with a toothpick. Bake at 450° for 10 minutes.

MICROWAVE METHOD:
Prepare as above. Microwave snacks, uncovered, HIGH, 2 snacks, 20-25 seconds; 6 snacks, 1 minute; 12 snacks, 1 minute 45 seconds-2 minutes.

Happy Hour Pizza

1 jar (14 oz.) **RAGÚ® Pizza Quick Sauce, with Mushrooms**
24 slices cocktail rye bread (2″ diameter), lightly toasted
6 slices cooked, crumbled bacon
⅔ cup (about 3 oz.) crumbled blue cheese
¼ cup sliced Spanish olives

Preheat broiler. Spoon 1 teaspoon **Pizza Quick Sauce** onto each bread slice. Evenly top with bacon, blue cheese and olives. Broil 5″ from heat 5-6 minutes or until cheese melts.

Makes 24 appetizers

Pastrami Pizzas

2 cups biscuit baking mix
½ cup cold water
1 cup pizza sauce
1 cup shredded mozzarella cheese
1 package **BUDDIG Smoked Sliced Pastrami**

Stir baking mix and water to a soft dough. Form dough into a ball on floured board and knead 5 times. Roll dough into a 15 × 9 inch rectangle. Cut into 3-inch squares; pinch edges to form rims. Spread each square with 1 tablespoon sauce; sprinkle with 1 tablespoon cheese and 1 tablespoon shredded pastrami. Bake on ungreased baking sheet 10 to 12 minutes in 425° oven.

Yield: 15 pizzas

Double Decker Pizza

1 loaf **RHODES™ Frozen Bread Dough**, thawed
2 green peppers, chopped
2 tomatoes, chopped
1 large onion, chopped
1¼ cups cut-up meat (salami, pepperoni, or cooked and drained sausage)
1 teaspoon Italian herbs (oregano, basil, marjoram)
½ teaspoon salt
1 cup shredded mozzarella cheese
½ cup grated Parmesan cheese
Softened butter or margarine
Sesame seeds

Cook green pepper, tomato and onion until onion is transparent. Add meat, herbs and salt; cook 5 minutes over low heat. Drain and cool.

Divide thawed dough into three equal parts. Roll each part into a rectangle 11 × 7-inches. Place one rectangle on a greased baking sheet. Spread with half the vegetable-meat mixture; sprinkle with half the mozzarella and Parmesan cheeses. Top with second rectangle of dough; repeat with remaining vegetable-meat mixture and cheese. Stretch third rectangle slightly; place on top. Pinch edges carefully together to seal. Brush top with butter; sprinkle with sesame seeds. Cover and let rise in a warm place about 1 hour.

Bake at 350°F. until a deep golden brown, about 40 to 45 minutes. Cut into slices. *Makes 6 to 8 servings*

Party Pizzas

4 English muffins
1 package **LAWRY'S® Extra Rich & Thick Spaghetti Sauce Mix**
1 can (1 lb.) tomatoes, cut in pieces
1 clove garlic, crushed
½ cup grated Cheddar or Parmesan cheese
2 tablespoons minced anchovy fillets or 1 pound crumbled cooked pork sausage (optional)

Split the muffins in half using fork. Broil to a light brown. Meanwhile, combine the **Extra Rich & Thick Spaghetti Sauce Mix**, tomatoes and crushed garlic. Stir thoroughly. Bring to a boil. Cover and simmer 20 minutes. Place 2 tablespoons sauce on each muffin half. Sprinkle with the cheese and anchovy or sausage, if desired. Broil until bubbling and brown. Cut each muffin half in fourths and serve hot. *Makes 32 pieces*

Beef Pepper Pizza

1 12½-oz. pkg. **APPIAN WAY® Pizza—Regular**
1 2½-oz. jar **ARMOUR® Star Sliced Dried Beef**, shredded
1 2½-oz. jar sliced mushrooms, drained
1 green pepper, sliced into rings
1 cup (4 oz.) shredded mozzarella cheese

Heat oven to 425°. Prepare pizza dough according to package directions; cover with sauce. Sprinkle with dried beef, mushrooms, green pepper and cheese. Bake at 425°, 18 to 20 minutes or until crust is golden brown.

3 to 4 servings, or cut into small pieces and serve as appetizer snacks

Tortilla Pizzas

Salad oil
8 **VAN DE KAMP'S® Corn Tortillas**
2 lbs. ground chuck
1 medium onion, minced
1 garlic clove, minced
¼ lb. mushrooms, chopped
1 can (2¼ oz.) chopped ripe olives
1 can (6 oz.) tomato paste
1¼ cups water
1 tsp. salt
1 package taco seasoning mix
½ lb. shredded Cheddar or mozzarella cheese
Grated Parmesan or Romano cheese

In a skillet, heat about 1 inch of salad oil. Fry tortillas, turning occasionally until lightly browned, about 1 minute. Drain on paper towel. Cook ground meat, onion, garlic, and mushrooms in a frying pan until meat is browned. Add olives, tomato paste, water, salt, and seasoning mix, and cook over low heat, stirring occasionally for about 5 minutes more. Place tortillas flat on baking sheets. Top each tortilla with about 4 tablespoons of the meat mixture, then with 3 tablespoons of the Cheddar cheese. Sprinkle lightly with Parmesan cheese. Bake in 425°F. oven for 10 minutes, or until cheese melts. *Makes 8 tortilla pizzas*

Lender's® Bagels

Lender's® Bagelettes

Tuna Toppers

Spread a **LENDER'S® Bagelette** with tunafish salad; top with thinly sliced red onion.

Blushing Lender's® Bagelette

Spread a **LENDER'S® Bagelette** with mayonnaise; top with thinly sliced turkey breast and diced pimiento.

Beefy Lender's® Bagelette

Spread a **LENDER'S® Bagelette** with mayonnaise mixed with drained horseradish; top with thinly sliced roast beef.

Gold Coin Lender's® Bagelette

Spread a **LENDER'S® Bagelette** with mustard; top with thin slices of narrow salami.

Melting Lender's® Bagelette

Spread a **LENDER'S® Bagelette** with Russian dressing; top with sliced tomato and Swiss cheese; heat until cheese melts.

Syrian Chicken Snacks

1 can (4¾ ounces) **UNDERWOOD® Chunky Chicken Spread**
2 tablespoons chopped celery
2 tablespoons chopped onion
3 small loaves Syrian (pita) bread (3 inches in diameter)
½ cup shredded Cheddar cheese

In a bowl, mix together chunky chicken spread, celery and onion. Split bread in half horizontally to make 6 flat slices. Spread each with chicken mixture and top with shredded cheese. Broil 3 to 5 minutes, until filling is hot and cheese is melted. Cut into quarters.

Makes 24 snacks

Continental Snacks

6 frozen **SARA LEE Individual Cinnamon Raisin** OR **Individual Apple** OR **Individual Cheese Danish**
Sliced Swiss cheese, cut into triangles
Sliced Cheddar cheese, cut into triangles
Thin sliced ham, cut into triangles

Warm Danish according to package directions. Place triangles of cheese on Cinnamon Raisin OR Apple Danish; OR place triangles of ham on Cheese Danish. *Makes 6 servings*

Danish 'n Eggs

6 frozen **SARA LEE Individual Cinnamon Raisin Danish***
6 poached eggs
½ cup grated Cheddar cheese

Warm Danish according to package directions. Place Danish on plates. Place egg on each Danish; top each serving with about 1 tablespoon cheese. *Makes 6 servings*

*Individual Apple or Individual Cheese Danish may be substituted.

Morton Salt

Homemade Tortilla Chips

3 cups flour
1 cup yellow cornmeal
4 teaspoons baking powder
1 tablespoon shortening
1 egg, beaten
1 cup water
Oil
MORTON® Popcorn Salt

Up to 1 Week or Day Before Serving: In large bowl, mix flour, cornmeal, and baking powder. Mix in shortening with fork. Stir in egg and water to form a stiff dough. Knead 5 minutes. Divide into 4 parts. Roll each into a 10-inch square, about ⅛-inch thick; cut into 2-inch squares. Divide each square into 2 triangles. Fry in 1-inch hot oil (about 360°F.) about 2 minutes, or until golden on both sides. Drain on paper towels. Sprinkle with popcorn salt. Cool. Store in airtight containers or plastic bags.

Just Before Serving: Place tortilla chips in lined basket or on decorative plate. *Makes about 1½ pounds or 200 chips*

Crescent-Easy Pretzels

8-oz. can **PILLSBURY Refrigerated Quick Crescent Dinner Rolls**
1 egg, beaten
Salt or coarse salt
KRAFT Pure Prepared Mustard

Heat oven to 375°F. Separate dough into 4 rectangles. Firmly press perforations to seal. Cut each rectangle lengthwise into 4 equal pieces; shape each into a 15-inch rope. Place each rope on ungreased cookie sheet, forming a pretzel shape. Brush each pretzel with beaten egg; sprinkle with salt. Bake at 375°F. for 8 to 12 minutes or until golden brown. Serve hot with mustard.

16 pretzels

High Altitude—Above 3500 Feet: No change.

NUTRITION INFORMATION PER SERVING
SERVING SIZE: ⅛ of recipe

Calories	110	Percent U.S. RDA Per Serving	
Protein	3 g	Protein	4%
Carbohydrate	13 g	Vitamin A	*
Fat	5 g	Thiamine	6%
Sodium	715 mg	Riboflavin	4%
Potassium	45 mg	Niacin	4%
		Calcium	*
		Iron	4%

*Contains less than 2% of the U.S. RDA of this nutrient.

PILLSBURY BAKE-OFF® recipe

San Giorgio®
Fried Pasta Croutons

2 cups **SAN GIORGIO® Shell Macaroni, Ditalini, Twirls,** etc.
Cooking oil
¼ cup grated Parmesan cheese
¼ teaspoon garlic salt

Cook pasta according to package directions; drain well. Dry on paper towel. Fry pasta, ½ cup at a time, in deep fat fryer or in deep oil in fry pan at 375° for about 2 minutes or until golden brown. Stir to separate. Drain on paper towels. While hot, toss with Parmesan cheese and garlic salt or herbs as suggested below. Cool. Store in airtight container. Use in salads or as garnish for casseroles.

VARIATIONS:

- Substitute ¼ teaspoon onion salt for garlic salt.
- Omit cheese and sprinkle hot pasta pieces with onion salt or garlic salt.
- Fry pasta, do not season. Use as dipper for your favorite dips and sauces.

NONE SUCH®
Granola Snack

½ cup creamy or crunchy peanut butter
¼ cup honey
¼ cup vegetable oil
2 tablespoons firmly packed brown sugar
1 (9-ounce) package **NONE SUCH® Condensed Mincemeat**
2 cups quick-cooking oats
1 cup dry-roasted peanuts

Preheat oven to 250°. In large saucepan, combine peanut butter, honey, vegetable oil and sugar; blend well. Break mincemeat into small pieces; add to peanut butter mixture. Boil briskly 1 minute, stirring constantly. Remove from heat. Add oats and peanuts; mix well. Spoon into 13 × 9-inch baking pan. Bake 45 minutes, stirring after 15 minutes and 30 minutes. Cool. Break into chunks. Store in tightly covered container.   *Makes 6½ cups*

Tip: To refreshen Granola Snack, place on baking sheet and bake at 250° for 10 minutes. Cool.

Super Simple Granola

3 cups **3 MINUTE BRAND® Oats** (we prefer
  Old Fashioned)
½ cup raisins
½ cup sunflower nuts
½ cup slivered almonds
½ cup chopped pecans
½ cup wheat germ
½ cup coconut
½ cup vegetable oil
⅓ cup honey

Combine all ingredients except oil and honey in a large mixing bowl. Mix oil and honey together; pour over oat mixture. Mix well. Spread into two 15 × 10 × 1-inch baking pans. Bake in a 300°F oven about 20 minutes, stirring once. Remove from pan when cool. Store in a tightly covered container.
                    Makes about 6 cups

Domino®
Crunchy Granola

4 cups rolled oats
⅓ cup wheat germ
⅓ cup shredded coconut
⅓ cup nonfat dry milk
1 cup slivered almonds
1 cup raisins
⅓ cup oil
¾ cup **DOMINO® Liquid Brown Sugar**
1 teaspoon vanilla

Preheat oven to 350°F. Spread the rolled oats in an ungreased 13 × 19-inch pan. Heat oats in oven for 10 minutes. Combine wheat germ, coconut, dry milk, almonds and raisins with oats in baking pan. Add oil, **DOMINO® Liquid Brown Sugar** and vanilla. Bake at 350°F for 20 to 25 minutes, stirring often to brown evenly. Cool. Stir mixture until crumbly. Store in tightly covered container in refrigerator.   *Makes about 6 cups*

Washington
Potato Skins

6 large (4 to 5 lbs.) **WASHINGTON RUSSET Potatoes**
Oil
¼ cup flour
Seasoned salt to taste

Scrub potatoes; rub lightly with oil. Pierce with fork. Bake at 400°F. 50 to 60 minutes or until tender. Cool. Cut potatoes in half lengthwise; scoop out pulp leaving ¼-inch shell. Pulp may be used for mashed potatoes or reserved for other use. Cut shells crosswise into 1-inch strips. Dip in flour; shake off excess. Deep-fry in oil heated to 375° F. 2 minutes or until lightly browned. Drain on absorbent paper towels. Sprinkle to taste with seasoned salt. Serve as an appetizer or accompany with dairy sour cream and minced green onion for dipping if desired.
                    Makes about 60 potato skins

To Reheat: Place fried skins on baking sheet. Bake at 375° F. about 10 minutes.

Favorite recipe from the **Washington State Potato Commission**

Finlandia Cheese Sticks

1 pkg. refrigerator crescent rolls
1 egg, beaten
1½ cups shredded **FINLANDIA Swiss Cheese**

Place perforated strips of refrigerator dough side by side and seal edges to form a large rectangle. Brush egg over surface of dough and sprinkle generously with cheese. Cut into sticks about 4 × 1 in. Place sticks on baking sheet and bake at 400 deg. 15 min. or until cheese is puffy and golden.

Note: Puff pastry or pie pastry dough may be substituted for the rolls.

Cheese Straws

2 cups (8 ozs.) shredded **CRACKER BARREL Brand
  Sharp Natural Cheddar Cheese**
⅓ cup **PARKAY Margarine**
1 teaspoon Worcestershire sauce
¼ teaspoon salt
1 cup flour

Heat oven to 375°. Thoroughly blend cheese and margarine; stir in Worcestershire sauce and salt. Add flour; mix well. Roll dough between two sheets of waxed paper to ⅛-inch thickness; cut into 3 × 1-inch strips. Place on lightly greased cookie sheets. Bake at 375°, 12 minutes.   *3 dozen*

Cheese Sticks

2 sticks pie crust mix (or 1 pkg. double crust pie mix)
1 cup shredded sharp natural cheddar cheese
1 Tbsp. **BALTIMORE SPICE OLD BAY Seasoning**

Prepare pie crust according to package instructions, mixing in cheese and **OLD BAY**. Roll dough on lightly floured surface to 12″ × 8″ rectangle. Cut into 3″ × ½″ strips. Bake on lightly greased baking sheet at 425° for 10-12 minutes.

Mexican Pick-Up Sticks

2 cans (3 oz. each) **DURKEE French Fried Onions**
1 can (7 oz.) **DURKEE Potato Sticks**
2 cups Spanish peanuts
⅓ cup butter or margarine, melted
1 pkg. (1⅛ oz.) **DURKEE Taco Seasoning Mix**

Combine first three ingredients and place in a 9 × 13-inch baking dish. Drizzle with melted butter; stir to combine. Sprinkle with Taco seasoning and mix well. Bake at 250° for 45 minutes. Stir every 15 minutes. *Makes approximately 2 quarts*

Traditional Chex® Party Mix

½ cup butter or margarine
1¼ teaspoons seasoned salt
4½ teaspoons Worcestershire sauce
2 cups **CORN CHEX® Cereal**
2 cups **RICE CHEX® Cereal**
2 cups **BRAN CHEX® Cereal**
2 cups **WHEAT CHEX® Cereal**
1 cup salted mixed nuts

Preheat oven to 250°. Heat butter in large shallow roasting pan (about 15 × 10 × 2-inches) in oven until melted. Remove. Stir in seasoned salt and Worcestershire sauce. Add **CHEX®** and nuts. Mix until all pieces are coated. Heat in oven 1 hour. Stir every 15 minutes. Spread on absorbent paper to cool.

Makes about 9 cups

Crunchy Fruit Munch

3 quarts freshly popped **JOLLY TIME® Pop Corn**
2 cups natural cereal with raisins
¾ cup dried apricots, chopped
¼ teaspoon salt
⅓ cup butter or margarine
¼ cup honey

Preheat oven to 300 degrees F. Combine first four ingredients in large baking pan; set aside. In small saucepan, combine butter or margarine and honey. Cook over low heat until butter or margarine is melted. Pour over pop corn mixture, tossing lightly until well coated. Place in oven. Bake 30 minutes, stirring occasionally. Store in tightly covered container up to 2 weeks.

Makes 3 quarts

Cheesy Sesame Crunch

½ cup flour
1 tablespoon cornstarch
1 teaspoon onion salt
½ cup water
1 tablespoon Worcestershire sauce
¼ teaspoon **TABASCO® Pepper Sauce**
¼ cup sesame seed
1 6-oz. box **BROWNBERRY® Cheddar Cheese Croutons**

In medium mixing bowl, combine all ingredients except croutons; beat with rotary beater. Fold in croutons until well coated. Spread on buttered 15½ × 10½ × 1-inch baking pan. Bake 350° for 20 minutes, stirring occasionally. Serve hot or cold as a snack.

Jolly Time® Party Mix

2 quarts popped **JOLLY TIME® Pop Corn**
2 cups slim pretzel sticks
2 cups cheese curls
¼ cup butter or margarine
1 tablespoon Worcestershire Sauce
½ teaspoon garlic salt
½ teaspoon seasoned salt

In a shallow baking pan, mix popped corn, pretzel sticks and cheese curls. Melt butter or margarine in small saucepan and stir in seasonings. Pour over dry mixture and mix well. Bake at 250 degrees F. for 45 minutes, stirring several times.

Makes 2½ quarts

Note: 1 cup dry roasted peanuts may be added.

Dried Fruit Trail Mix

½ cup coarsely chopped **DIAMOND® Walnuts**
½ cup flaked or shredded coconut
⅓ cup sunflower seeds
1 cup **SUNSWEET® Pitted Prunes**
½ cup **SUNSWEET® Dried Apricots**
½ cup **SUNSWEET® Dried Apples**

Combine walnuts, coconut and sunflower seeds in shallow baking pan. Bake at 350°F. about 10 min. until lightly toasted, stirring once or twice. Cool. Snip prunes, apricots and apples into small pieces. Combine with toasted mixture. Store in covered container.

Makes 3 cups

Toasty O's Snack Mix

3 cups **MALT-O-MEAL® Toasty O's Cereal**
½ cup pretzel sticks, broken
2 cups miniature shredded wheats, cut in half
½ cup nuts or peanuts
6 Tbsp. Butter or margarine, melted
1 Tbsp. Worcestershire sauce
½ tsp. garlic powder
½ tsp. onion salt

In a small bowl, combine **Toasty O's Cereal**, shredded wheat, pretzels, and nuts. To the melted butter add Worcestershire sauce, garlic powder, and onion salt. Pour gradually over cereal mixture stirring constantly to blend evenly. Spread in shallow baking pan. Bake in a 250° oven for 45 minutes or until lightly toasted. Stir occasionally, let cool. To keep fresh, store in an airtight container.

Barbecue Rancho Snacks
(Low Calorie)

¼ cup butter or margarine
3 tablespoons barbecue sauce
¾ teaspoon garlic salt
¼ teaspoon barbecue spice
4 cups **SPOON SIZE Shredded Wheat**

Melt butter or margarine in a 13 × 9 × 2-inch baking pan. Blend in next three ingredients. Add **SPOON SIZE Shredded Wheat**. Cook and stir gently until cereal is well coated. Bake in a preheated moderate oven (350°F.) 15 to 18 minutes or until lightly browned and crisp. Cool. *Makes 4 cups*

Calories: About 6 per Barbecue Rancho Snack

Chinatown Munch

2 cups **MALT-O-MEAL® Puffed Rice**
¾ cup roasted salted peanuts
¾ cup sesame sticks
½ cup roasted, salted sunflower seeds
3 tablespoons salad oil
1½ tablespoons soy sauce
¼ teaspoon ground ginger

Combine **Puffed Rice**, peanuts, sesame sticks and sunflower seeds in a large bowl. Blend oil, soy sauce and ginger. Toss with **Puffed Rice** mixture. Spread on a rimmed baking sheet. Bake in a 250°F. oven for 30 minutes. Store in an airtight container.
Makes about 4 cups

Teriyaki Trail Mix

⅓ cup **KIKKOMAN Teriyaki Sauce**
2 tablespoons vegetable oil
1 cup pecan halves
1 cup walnut halves
2 cups toasted oat cereal (like **CHEERIOS**)
1 cup shredded coconut
¾ cup sunflower seed
½ cup blanched slivered almonds
1 cup raisins

Combine teriyaki sauce and oil in large bowl; stir in pecans and walnuts until thoroughly coated. Let stand 10 minutes; stir occasionally. Add next 4 ingredients; toss together to combine and coat thoroughly. Turn out onto large shallow baking pan or cookie sheet; spread mixture out evenly. Bake at 250°F. 15 minutes. Remove from oven and stir gently. Bake 15 minutes longer. Remove from oven; stir in raisins and let stand in pan until thoroughly cooled. Store in tightly covered container.

Crispy Snacks

2 quarts water
2 teaspoons salt
1 tablespoon oil
3⅔ cups **AMERICAN BEAUTY® CURLY-RONI®** or
    1¾ cups **ELBO-RONI®**
Oil for deep frying
Seasoning

Choose one of the following:
½ cup grated Parmesan cheese combined with
    2 teaspoons Italian seasoning
    2 teaspoons Mexican seasoning
    2 teaspoons seasoned salt
    2 teaspoons onion salt

Boil water in large deep pot with salt and 1 tablespoon oil (to prevent boiling over). Add **CURLY-RONI®**, stir to separate. Cook uncovered after water returns to a full rolling boil for 10 to 11 minutes. Stir occasionally. Drain and rinse under hot water. Pat dry with paper towels.

In medium saucepan or deep fryer, heat oil to 375°F. Fry cooked **CURLY-RONI®**, ½ cup at a time, for 2 to 3 minutes until crispy and slightly golden. Do not overcook. Stir to separate while frying. Spread on paper towels to drain; separate if necessary. Sprinkle with desired seasoning. *8 servings*

High Altitude—Above 3500 Feet: Cooking times may need to be increased slightly for **CURLY-RONI®**. Heat oil to 360°F. and fry 2½ to 3½ minutes.

NUTRITION INFORMATION PER SERVING			
SERVING SIZE: ⅛ of recipe		PERCENT U.S. RDA	
Calories	155	PER SERVING	
Protein	7g	Protein	10
Carbohydrate	22g	Vitamin A	—
Fat	4g	Vitamin C	—
Sodium	413mg	Thiamin	9
Potassium	69mg	Riboflavin	8
		Niacin	5
		Calcium	11
		Iron	5

Nutritional information does not include the oil used for frying.

Scrimmage

½ cup butter or margarine
4 cups **SPOON SIZE Shredded Wheat**
1 cup mixed nuts
¼ cup granulated sugar
1½ teaspoons ground cinnamon
½ cup **DROMEDARY Chopped Dates**

In large skillet melt butter or margarine. Stir in next two ingredients; sauté over medium heat until toasted, shaking skillet occasionally. Combine sugar and cinnamon. Toss with cereal mixture and dates; let cool. *Makes about 5½ cups*

Nutty Garlic Snacks

¾ cup finely chopped nuts
½ to 1½ teaspoons garlic salt
10-oz. can **HUNGRY JACK® Refrigerated Flaky Biscuits**
1 egg, slightly beaten
1½ cups roasted peanuts or nuts, if desired

(Continued)

(Continued)

Heat oven to 375°F. Combine chopped nuts and garlic salt. Separate dough into 10 biscuits; cut each into 4 pieces. Roll each biscuit piece into a ball; dip top and sides in beaten egg, then in nut mixture. Place on ungreased cookie sheets. Bake at 375°F. for 9 to 12 minutes or until light golden brown; cool. If desired, toss snacks with roasted peanuts to serve. *40 snacks*

Tip: To make ahead, prepare, cover and refrigerate up to 2 hours; bake as directed.

High Altitude—Above 3500 Feet: No change.

NUTRITION INFORMATION PER SERVING
SERVING SIZE: 1/10 of recipe

		Percent U.S. RDA	
Calories	150	Per Serving	
Protein	4 g	Protein	6%
Carbohydrate	15 g	Vitamin A	*
Fat	8 g	Vitamin C	*
Sodium	390 mg	Thiamine	8%
Potassium	70 mg	Riboflavin	6%
		Niacin	4%
		Calcium	*
		Iron	4%

*Contains less than 2% of the U.S. RDA of this nutrient.

PILLSBURY BAKE-OFF® recipe

Chow Mein Noodle Party Snacks

1 can (3 ozs.) **LA CHOY® Fancy Chow Mein Noodles**
2 tablespoons melted butter
2 drops hot pepper sauce
¼ teaspoon **LA CHOY® Soy Sauce**
¼ teaspoon celery salt
¼ teaspoon onion powder

Put Chow Mein Noodles in shallow pan. Combine remaining ingredients; pour over Chow Mein Noodles, stirring gently with a fork. Heat in a 250° oven for 30 minutes, stirring occasionally. Serve warm or cold. Can be stored in a tightly covered container for several days.

Praline® Popcorn Crunch

10 cups popped corn
1½ cups whole pecans
½ cup slivered almonds
1⅓ cups sugar
1 cup butter
¼ cup **PRALINE® Liqueur**
¼ cup light corn syrup
1 tablespoon **PRALINE® Liqueur**
¼ teaspoon salt

Heat oven to 325°F. Butter baking sheet and large bowl. Toast pecans and almonds until light brown, about 12-15 minutes. Mix popped corn and nuts in large bowl.
  Combine sugar, butter, ¼ cup **PRALINE® Liqueur** and corn syrup in heavy 2-quart saucepan. Cook over medium-high heat, stirring occasionally to 275°F., or until small amount dropped into very cold water reaches soft crack stage (separates into hard, but not brittle, threads). Remove from heat, quickly stir in 1 tablespoon **PRALINE® Liqueur** and salt. Pour over popped corn and nuts, mixing until evenly coated. Immediately spread mixture on baking sheet. Let stand about one hour. Break into bite-size pieces. *Makes about 14 cups*

Gold'n Nut Crunch!

1 can (12 ounces) **FISHER® Mixed Nuts** or 1 jar (12 ounces) **FISHER® Dry Roasted Peanuts**
¼ cup **LAND O LAKES® Sweet Cream Butter**, melted
¼ cup grated Parmesan cheese
¼ teaspoon garlic powder
¼ teaspoon ground oregano
¼ teaspoon celery salt
4 cups **GOLDEN GRAHAMS® Cereal**

Heat oven to 300°. Mix nuts and butter in medium bowl until well coated. Add cheese, garlic powder, oregano and celery salt; toss until well coated. Spread in ungreased jelly roll pan, 15½ × 10½ × 1 inch. Bake, stirring occasionally, 15 minutes. Stir in cereal; cool. Store in airtight container. *About 6½ cups snack*

SKILLET METHOD:
Heat butter in heavy 10-inch skillet until melted. Add remaining ingredients; stir until well coated. Heat over low heat, stirring occasionally, 5 minutes; cool.

Perky Party Mix

1½ cups **"M&M's" Plain** or **Peanut Chocolate Candies**
3 cups thin pretzel sticks, broken in half
3 cups bite-size Cheddar cheese crackers
1½ cups raisins

Combine all ingredients. Serve as a snack.
Makes about 8 cups mix

Jif®
Double Peanut Snack Mix

4 cups sweet shredded oat cereal
1 cup peanuts
¼ cup butter or margarine
¼ cup **JIF® Creamy Peanut Butter**
1 teaspoon ground cinnamon

In large bowl, combine cereal and peanuts. In small saucepan heat butter or margarine, **JIF®**, and cinnamon over low heat till butter and **JIF®** are melted. Stir till blended. Slowly pour over cereal mixture, mixing well. Spread out in a 13 × 9 × 2-inch baking pan. Bake in 350° oven 10 to 12 minutes; stir occasionally. Cool.
Makes about 4 cups

Peanut Butter Party Mix

2 tablespoons **MAZOLA®/NUCOA® Margarine**
⅓ cup **SKIPPY® Creamy Peanut Butter**
2 cups bite-size toasted wheat biscuits
2 cups bite-size toasted rice biscuits
¼ cup dry-roasted peanuts

In large skillet melt margarine over low heat. Stir in peanut butter until thoroughly mixed. Toss cereal and nuts in mixture until coated. Remove from heat. Spread on ungreased cookie sheet. Bake in 375°F oven 8 minutes or until golden brown. Drain on paper towels.

Makes about 4 cups

On the Run Trail Mix

3 cups **QUAKER® 100% Natural Cereal**
⅔ cup chopped walnuts
⅓ cup firmly packed brown sugar
¼ cup butter or margarine
3 tablespoons honey
1 tablespoon grated orange peel

Heat oven to 325°F. Combine cereal and nuts in large bowl. Combine brown sugar, butter and honey in small saucepan; cook over low heat, stirring occasionally until smooth. Stir in orange peel. Pour over cereal mixture; mix well. Spread into lightly greased 13 × 9-inch baking pan. Bake at 325°F. for 20 to 22 minutes or until golden brown, stirring occasionally. Remove mixture to ungreased cookie sheet or aluminum foil; cool completely. Break into pieces. Store in tightly covered container.

Makes about 6 cups

Crisco

Snacking-Good Nuts

⅓ cup **CRISCO® Shortening**
1½ teaspoons chili powder
1 teaspoon Worcestershire sauce
½ teaspoon cayenne pepper
½ teaspoon garlic salt
2 cups cashews
2 cups pecans

Preheat oven to 300°. In 11×7×1½-inch baking pan, melt the **CRISCO®** in the 300° oven. When melted, stir in the chili powder, Worcestershire sauce, cayenne, and garlic salt. Add the cashews and pecans and toss to coat the nuts. Spread nuts evenly in the baking pan. Bake at 300° for 20 to 25 minutes, stirring once or twice. Sprinkle the nuts with additional salt, if desired.

Makes about 4 cups nuts

Coffee Glazed Pecans

1½ cups pecans
¼ cup sugar
2 measuring tablespoons water
2 measuring teaspoons **TASTER'S CHOICE Instant Freeze-Dried Coffee**
¼ measuring teaspoon cinnamon

In large skillet or electric skillet*, combine pecans, sugar, water, **TASTER'S CHOICE** and cinnamon; bring to a boil over medium heat, stirring constantly. Boil 3 minutes, stirring con-

stantly until pecans are well glazed. Spread on waxed paper to cool.

Makes: 1½ cups glazed pecans

***Note:** In electric skillet, heat all ingredients approximately 4 minutes at 225°F., stirring constantly.

Oriental Almonds

1½ tablespoons butter or margarine
1½ tablespoons Worcestershire sauce
1 teaspoon salt
¼ teaspoon cinnamon
⅛ teaspoon chili powder
Dash hot pepper sauce
1 package (10 ounces) **BLUE DIAMOND® Blanched Whole Almonds** (2 cups)

Melt butter in two-quart baking dish in a 300 degree F. oven. Stir in Worcestershire sauce, salt, cinnamon, chili powder and hot pepper sauce. Add almonds; stir until completely coated. Bake, stirring occasionally, 15 minutes or until almonds are crisp.

Makes 2 cups

SKIPPY®

Quick Peanutty Popcorn Balls

½ cup light corn syrup
¼ cup sugar
¾ cup **SKIPPY® Creamy** or **Super Chunk Peanut Butter**
2 quarts plain popped corn

In 1-quart saucepan mix corn syrup and sugar. Cook over medium heat, stirring constantly, until mixture comes to boil and sugar is completely dissolved. Remove from heat. Stir in peanut butter until smooth. Immediately pour mixture over popped corn in large bowl. Stir until evenly coated. Grease hands and shape into 8 (2½-inch) balls.

Makes 8

SUE BEE HONEY

Greek Dates

½ cup **SUE BEE® Honey**
½ cup chopped toasted almonds
½ cup chopped walnuts
½ cup diced orange peel
1 pound pitted dates
Granulated sugar

Mix honey, nuts and orange peel. Stuff dates with mixture, and roll in sugar. To preserve freshness, wrap dates individually in plastic wrap.

Acknowledgments

The Editors of CONSUMER GUIDE® wish to thank the companies and organizations listed for use of their recipes and artwork. For further information contact the following:

Alaska Seafood Mktg. Inst. *see* Pacific Kitchen

Almadén Vineyards
San Jose, CA 95150

Amaretto di Amore®, *see* Wile, Julius

Amber Brand Deviled Smithfield Ham
The Smithfield Ham and Products Co.
Smithfield, VA 23430

American Beauty®, *see* Pillsbury Co., The

American Egg Board
1460 Renaissance
Park Ridge, IL 60068

American Soybean Association
777 Craig Rd.
St. Louis, MO 63141

Angostura®—A-W Brands, Inc.
Carteret, NJ 07008

Appian Way®, *see* Armour and Co.

Argo®/Kingsford's®, *see* Best Foods

Armour and Co.
Phoenix, AZ 85077

Arnold Sorensin, Inc.
Hackensack, NJ 07601

Aspen™—Spar, Inc.
803 Jefferson Hwy.
New Orleans, LA 70152

Atalanta/Krakus/Polka—Atalanta Corp.
17 Varick St.
New York, NY 10013

Azteca Corn Products Corp.
4850 S. Austin
Chicago, IL 60638-1491

B&B Liqeur, *see* Wile, Julius

BinB®, *see* Clorox Co., The

Baltimore Spice Co., The
P.O. Box 5858
Baltimore, MD 21208

Banquet Foods Corp.
Ballwin, MO 63011

Bays English Muffin Corp.
500 N. Michigan Ave.
Chicago, IL 60611

Bénédictine, *see* Wile, Julius

Bertolli U.S.A.
P.O. Box 931
So. San Francisco, CA 94080

Best Foods
Englewood Cliffs, NJ 07632

Bisquick®, *see* General Mills, Inc.

Blue Diamond®—Calif. Almond Growers Exch.
P.O. Box 1768
Sacramento, Ca 95808

Blue Ribbon®—Continental Nut Co.
Chico, CA 95927

Bolla—The Jos. Garneau Co.
P.O. Box 1080
Louisville, KY 40201

Booth Fisheries Corp.
2 North Riverside Plaza
Chicago, IL 60606

Borden Inc.
180 E. Broad St.
Columbus, OH 43215

Bordo Products Co.
2825 Sheffield Ave.
Chicago, IL 60657

Breakstone's®, *see* Kraft, Inc.—Dairy Group

Breyers®, *see* Kraft, Inc.—Dairy Group

Bridgford Foods Corp.
1308 N. Patt St.
Anaheim, CA 92801

Brownberry
Oconomowoc, WI 53066

Buddig, Carl, & Co.
11914 S. Peoria St.
Chicago, IL 60643

Bumble Bee®, *see* Castle & Cooke

Butter Buds®, *see* Cumberland Packing

Butterball®, *see* Swift & Co.

Calavo Growers of California
Box 3486, Terminal Annex
Los Angeles, CA 90051

California Table Grape Commission, *see* Pacific Kitchen

Campbell Soup Co.
Camden, NJ 08101

Castle & Cooke Foods
50 California St.
San Francisco, CA 94119

Cheez-Ola®—Fisher Cheese Co.
Wapakoneta, OH 45895

Cheez Whiz, *see* Kraft, Inc.

Chef Boy-Ar-Dee®—American Home Foods
685 Third Ave.
New York, NY 10017

Chex® Cereals, *see* Ralston Purina Co.

Christian Brothers® The—Fromm and Sichel, Inc.
San Francisco, CA 94120

Claussen, *see* Oscar Mayer Foods Corp.

Clorox Co., The
Oakland, CA 94623

Coca-Cola Co., The
P.O. Drawer 1734
Atlanta, GA 30301

Coco Casa™, *see* Holland House Brands

Colonial Sugars, Inc.
Mobile, AL 36633

Cookin' Good™—Showell Farms, Inc.
Showell, MD 21862

Corn Diggers, *see* Nabisco Brands, Inc.

Country Smoked Meats Inc.
P.O. Box 981-E
Wooster, OH 44691

Cracker Barrel, *see* Kraft, Inc.

Crisco®, *see* Procter & Gamble Co.

Cumberland Packing Corp.
Brooklyn, NY 11205

Dannon Co., Inc., The
22-11 38th Avenue
Long Island City, NY 11101

Darigold—Consolidated Dairy Products Co.
635 Elliott Ave. W.
Seattle, WA 98109

Del Monte Corp.
P.O. Box 3575
San Francisco, CA 94119

Deming's, *see* Peter Pan Seafoods

Denmark Cheese Assn.
4415 W. Harrison
Hillside, IL 60163

Diamond®, *see* Sun-Diamond

Domino®—Amstar Corp.
1251 Avenue of the Americas
New York, NY 10020

Dorman, N., & Co.
Syosset, NY 11791

Double Q, *see* Peter Pan Seafoods

Dromedary, *see* Nabisco Brands, Inc.

Droste®, *see* Wile, Julius

Dubonnet—Schenley Affiliated Brands
888 Seventh Ave.
New York, NY 10106

Dunphy's, *see* Wile, Julius

Durkee Foods - Div. of SCM Corp.
Strongsville, OH 44136

Eckrich, Peter, & Sons, Inc.
Fort Wayne, IN 46801

Escort, *see* Nabisco Brands, Inc.

Figaro Co., The
111 Manufacturing St.
Dallas, TX 75207

Filippo Berio—Berio Importing Corp.
109 Montgomery Ave.
Scarsdale, NY 10583

Finlandia Cheese, *see* Atalanta Corp.

Finlandia® Vodka—The Buckingham Corp.
620 5th Ave.
New York, NY 10020

Fisher Nut Company
St. Paul, MN 55164

Fleischmann's®, *see* Nabisco Brands

Florida Dept. of Natural Resources
3900 Commonwealth Blvd.
Tallahassee, FL 32303

French, R.T., Co.
Rochester, NY 14609

Frito-Lay, Inc.
Dallas, TX 75235

Gallo Salame
250 Brannan St.
San Francisco, CA 94107

Gebhardt Mexican Foods
San Antonio, TX 78285

General Mills, Inc.
Minneapolis, MN 55440

Gerber Products Co.
Fremont, MI 49412

Gilnettersbest, *see* Peter Pan Seafoods

Green Giant®, *see* Pillsbury Co., The

Gulf and South Atlantic Fisheries
5401 W. Kennedy Blvd.
Tampa, FL 33609

Harvest Brand®, *see* National Oats Co.

Heinz U.S.A.
Pittsburgh, PA 15212

Hellmann's®, *see* Best Foods

Herb-Ox®—The Pure Food Co.
Mamaroneck, NY 10543

Hi Ho Crackers®, *see* Sunshine Biscuits

Hidden Valley Original Ranch®, *see* Clorox Co., The

High Liner®—National Sea Products
Etibicoke, Ont. Canada M9C2Y3

High Sea®, *see* Robinson Canning Co.

Hillshire Farm®—Kahn's and Co.
3241 Spring Grove Ave.
Cincinnati, OH 45225

Hiram Walker Inc.
P.O. Box 33006
Detroit, MI 48232

Holland House Brands Co.
1125 Pleasant View Terrace
Ridgefield, NJ 07657

Holly Farms Poultry Industries, Inc.
Wilkesboro, NC 28697

Hormel, Geo. A., & Co.
Austin, MN 55912

Humpty Dumpty, *see* Peter Pan Seafoods

Hungry Jack®, *see* Pillsbury Co., The

Hunt-Wesson Kitchens
Fullerton, CA 92634

Imperial Sugar Co.
P.O. Box 50129
Dallas, TX 75250

International Multifoods
Eight & Marquette
Minneapolis, MN 55402

Irish Mist®—Heublein/Spirits
330 New Park Ave.
Hartford, CT 06101

Jacquin, Charles, et Cie, Inc.
2633 Trenton Ave.
Philadelphia, PA 19125

Jays Foods, Inc.
825 E. 99th St.
Chicago, IL 60628

Jeno's
Duluth, MN 55802

Jif®, *see* Procter & Gamble Co.

Jimmy Dean Meat Company, Inc.
1341 W. Mockingbird Ln.
Dallas, TX 75247

Johnnie Walker—Somerset Importers
1114 Avenue of the Americas
New York, NY 10036-7755

Jolly Time®—American Pop Corn Co.
Sioux City, IA 51102

Karo®, *see* Best Foods

Kaukauna®, *see* International Multifoods

Kellogg Company
Battle Creek, MI 49016

Kikkoman International, Inc.
50 California St.
San Francisco, CA 94111

King Oscar Fine Foods
Millburn, NJ 07041

Knox®, *see* Lipton, Thomas J.

Krakus, *see* Atalanta Corp.

Kraft, Inc.
Glenview, IL 60025

Kraft, Inc.—Dairy Group
P.O. Box 7830
Philadelphia, PA 19101

Kretschmer, *see* International Multifoods

La Choy Food Products
Archbold, OH 43502

La Fiesta™—Fiesta Foods, Inc.
310 W. Mockingbird
Dallas, TX 75247

Lawry's Foods, Inc.
570 W. Avenue 26
Los Angeles, CA 90065

Lay's®, *see* Frito-Lay, Inc.

Lea & Perrins, Inc.
Fair Lawn, NJ 07410

Lender's Bagel Bakery, Inc.
West Haven, CT 06516

Libby, McNeill & Libby, Inc.
200 S. Michigan Ave.
Chicago, IL 60604

Lindsay International Inc.
Visalia, CA 93277

Lipton, Thomas J., Inc.
Englewood Cliffs, NJ 07632

Louisiana Brand, *see* Robinson Canning Co.

M&M/Mars
Hackettstown, NJ 07840

Malt-O-Meal Co.
1520 TCF Towers
Minneapolis, MN 55402

Mazola®/Nucoa®, *see* Best Foods

Meadow Gold Dairies
1526 S. State St.
Chicago, IL 60605

Metaxa®, *see* Wile, Julius

Migliore®—Scheps Cheese
Haledon, NJ 07538

Milnot Company
P.O. Box 190
Litchfield, IL 62056

Minute Maid®—The Coca-Cola Co.
P.O. Box 2079
Houston, TX 77001

Morton Salt
110 N. Wacker Dr.
Chicago, IL 60606

Mrs. Paul's Kitchens, Inc.
5830 Henry Ave.
Philadelphia, PA 19128

Nabisco Brands, Inc.
625 Madison Ave.
New York, NY 10022

Nalley's Fine Foods Div.
Tacoma, WA 98411

National Hot Dog & Sausage Council
400 W. Madison
Chicago, IL 60606

National Marine Fisheries Service
3300 Whitehaven, NW
Washington, DC 20235

National Oats Co., Inc.
1515 H Ave. NE
Cedar Rapids, IA 52402

National Pecan Marketing Council
1800 Peachtree Rd., N.W.
Atlanta, GA 30309

Nestlé Co., The
White Plains, NY 10605

None Such®, see Borden Inc.

Nucoa®, see Best Foods

Old El Paso®, see Pet Inc.

Old London®, see Borden Inc.

Ore-Ida Foods, Inc.
Boise, ID 83707

Oscar Mayer Foods Corp.
Madison, WI 53707

Pacific Kitchen
300 Elliott Ave. W.
Seattle, WA 98119

Parkay, see Kraft, Inc.

Pepperidge Farm, Inc.
Norwalk, CT 06856

Pet, Inc.
St. Louis, MO 63166

Peter Pan Seafoods, Inc.
Dexter Horton Bldg.
Seattle, WA 98104

Philadelphia Brand, see Kraft, Inc.

Pillsbury Co., The
Minneapolis, MN 55402

Planters®, see Nabisco Brands, Inc.

Polka, see Atalanta Corp.

Pompelan, Inc.
4201 Pulaski Hwy.
Baltimore, MD 21224

Praline®, see Hiram Walker Inc.

Premium, see Nabisco Brands, Inc.

Procter & Gamble Co. Foods Div.
Cincinnati, OH 45202

Progresso Quality Foods
Rochelle Park, NJ 07662

Quaker Oats Co., The
Chicago, IL 60654

Ragú®—Chesebrough-Pond's Inc.
Trumbull, CT 06611

Ralston Purina Co.
St. Louis, MO 63188

Rath Packing Co., The
Waterloo, IA 50704

ReaLemon®, see Borden Inc.

Rhodes™—Dakota Bake-N-Serv, Inc.
Jamestown, ND 58401-0688

Robin Hood®, see International Multifoods

Robinson Canning Co., Inc.
Westwego, LA 70094

Romanoff®—Iroquois Grocery Products
111 High Ridge Rd.
Stamford, CT 06902

Roquefort Association, Inc.
41 E. 42nd St.
New York, NY 10017

Rosarita Mexican Foods Co.
Mesa, AZ 85201

San Giorgio-Skinner, Inc.
Hershey, PA 17033

Sara Lee, Kitchens of
Deerfield, IL 60015

Sargento Cheese Co. Inc.
Plymouth, WI 53073

Sealtest®, see Kraft—Dairy Group

Sesame Wheats, Nabisco Brands

Shoal Lake Wild Rice Ltd.
Keewatin, Ont., Canada POX 1CO

Skippy®, see Best Foods

Smucker, J.M., Co., The
Orrville, OH 44667

Snack Mate, see Nabisco Brands, Inc.

Snow's®, see Borden Inc.

Sociables, see Nabisco Brands, Inc.

South African Rock Lobster Serv. Corp.
70 Wall St.
New York, NY 10005

Southern Comfort Corp.
1220 N. Price Rd.
St. Louis, MO 63132

Spoon Size, see Nabisco Brands, Inc.

Star-Kist Foods, Inc.
Terminal Island, CA 90731

Stokely-Van Camp, Inc.
Indianapolis, IN 46206

Sue Bee®—Sioux Honey Assn.
Sioux City, IA 51102

Sun-Diamond Growers of California
San Ramon, CA 94583

Sun World, Inc.
5544 California Ave.
Bakersfield, CA 93309

Sunkist Growers, Inc.
Van Nuys, CA 91409

Sunshine Biscuits, Inc.
245 Park Ave.
New York, NY 10017

Sunsweet®, see Sun-Diamond

Swanson, see Campbell Soup Co.

Sweet 'N Low®, see Cumberland Packing

Sweetlite™—Batterlite Whitlock
P.O. Box 259
Springfield, IL 62705

Swift & Co.
Oak Brook, IL 60521

Tabasco®—McIlhenny Co.
Avery Island, LA 70513

Taster's Choice, see The Nestlé Co.

Tennessee Pride®—Qdom Sausage Co.
Madison, TN 37115

TexaSweet Citrus Advertising, Inc.
McAllen, TX 78501

3-Minute Brand®, see National Oats Co.
Inc.

Triscuit, see Nabisco Brands, Inc.

Tuna Research Foundation
1101 17th St., N.W.
Washington, DC 20036

Two Fingers®, see Hiram Walker Inc.

Uncle Ben's Foods
Houston, TX 77001

Underwood, Wm., Co.
Westwood, MA 02090

Van Camp's®, see Stokely-Van Camp

Van De Kamp's Frozen Foods
13100 Arctic Circle
Santa Fe Springs, CA 90670

Veg-All®—The Larsen Co.
520 N. Broadway
Green Bay, WI 54305

Velveeta, see Kraft, Inc.

Vienna Sausage Mfg. Co.
2501 N. Damen Ave.
Chicago, IL 60647

Virginia Dare Extract Co.
882 Third Ave.
Brooklyn, NY 11232

Wakefield®—Pacific Pearl Seafoods
1450 114th Ave. S.E.
Bellevue, WA 98004

Washington State Potato Comm., see
Pacific Kitchen

Wile, Julius, Sons & Co., Inc.
Lake Success, NY 11042

Wilson Foods Corp.
Oklahoma City, OK 73105

Wise®, see Borden Inc.

Wish-Bone®, see Lipton, Thomas J.

Wispride, see The Nestlé Co.

Wolf Brand Products
2929 Carlisle St.
Dallas, TX 75204

Wolff's®—The Birkett Mills
Penn Yan, NY 14527

Wright, E.H., Co., Inc.
Brentwood, TN 37027

Wyler's®, see Borden Inc.

Index